50 Holiday Feast Recipes for Home

By: Kelly Johnson

Table of Contents

- Roast Turkey with Cranberry Glaze
- Garlic and Herb Prime Rib
- Honey Glazed Ham
- Herb-Roasted Leg of Lamb
- Stuffed Cornish Hens
- Beef Wellington
- Vegan Lentil Loaf
- Mushroom Wellington
- Cranberry and Pecan Stuffed Acorn Squash
- Grilled Salmon with Dill Sauce
- Classic Beef Brisket
- Roasted Duck with Orange Sauce
- Herb-Crusted Pork Tenderloin
- Vegetarian Mushroom Gravy
- Creamy Butternut Squash Soup
- Shrimp Scampi
- Lemon Herb Roasted Chicken
- Garlic Mashed Potatoes
- Sweet Potato Casserole with Pecan Streusel
- Green Bean Almondine
- Roasted Brussels Sprouts with Balsamic Glaze
- Cranberry Orange Relish
- Classic Bread Stuffing
- Wild Rice Pilaf
- Pumpkin Risotto
- Garlic Parmesan Roasted Asparagus
- Creamed Spinach
- Apple Walnut Salad with Maple Vinaigrette
- Caesar Salad with Homemade Dressing
- Deviled Eggs with Bacon
- Cheese Platter with Assorted Crackers
- Fresh Dinner Rolls
- Cranberry Orange Scones
- Pumpkin Pie with Whipped Cream
- Pecan Pie

- Classic Apple Pie
- Chocolate Yule Log Cake
- Gingerbread Cookies
- Peppermint Bark
- Eggnog Cheesecake
- Linzer Cookies
- Bûche de Noël
- Cranberry Pistachio Biscotti
- Spiced Apple Cider
- Mulled Wine
- Festive Holiday Punch
- Sparkling Cranberry Mocktail
- Hot Chocolate with Marshmallows
- Cinnamon Spiced Nuts
- Assorted Holiday Truffles

Roast Turkey with Cranberry Glaze

Ingredients:

- 1 whole turkey (12-14 pounds)
- Salt and pepper, to taste
- 1 onion, quartered
- 1 lemon, quartered
- 4-6 sprigs fresh rosemary
- 4-6 sprigs fresh thyme
- 1 cup chicken or turkey broth

For the Cranberry Glaze:

- 1 cup cranberry sauce (homemade or store-bought)
- 1/4 cup orange juice
- 2 tablespoons honey
- 1 tablespoon Dijon mustard
- 1 teaspoon grated orange zest

Instructions:

Prepare the Turkey:
- Preheat your oven to 325°F (165°C).
- Remove the turkey from the refrigerator and let it sit at room temperature for about 30 minutes.
- Pat the turkey dry with paper towels. Season the cavity generously with salt and pepper.
- Stuff the cavity with quartered onion, lemon, rosemary, and thyme.

Truss and Season:
- Truss the turkey legs with kitchen twine to help the turkey cook evenly.
- Rub the outside of the turkey with olive oil and season generously with salt and pepper.

Roasting:
- Place the turkey on a roasting rack in a large roasting pan.
- Pour chicken or turkey broth into the bottom of the roasting pan.
- Cover the turkey loosely with aluminum foil.

Cooking the Turkey:

- Roast the turkey in the preheated oven for about 2 to 2.5 hours, basting occasionally with pan juices.
- Remove the foil during the last 30 minutes of cooking to allow the skin to brown.

Making the Cranberry Glaze:
- While the turkey is roasting, prepare the cranberry glaze.
- In a saucepan over medium heat, combine cranberry sauce, orange juice, honey, Dijon mustard, and orange zest.
- Stir and cook until the mixture is heated through and slightly thickened. Remove from heat.

Applying the Glaze:
- During the last 30 minutes of roasting, start brushing the cranberry glaze over the turkey every 10-15 minutes until the turkey reaches an internal temperature of 165°F (75°C) in the thickest part of the thigh.

Rest and Serve:
- Once done, transfer the turkey to a cutting board and tent loosely with foil. Let it rest for at least 20-30 minutes before carving.
- Serve the roast turkey with the remaining cranberry glaze on the side.

Enjoy your delicious roast turkey with cranberry glaze as the centerpiece of your holiday feast!

Garlic and Herb Prime Rib

Ingredients:

- 1 bone-in prime rib roast (about 5-6 pounds)
- 6 cloves garlic, minced
- 2 tablespoons fresh rosemary, finely chopped
- 2 tablespoons fresh thyme, finely chopped
- 2 tablespoons olive oil
- Salt and black pepper, to taste

For the Au Jus:

- Drippings from the cooked roast
- 1 cup beef broth
- 1/2 cup red wine (optional)
- Salt and pepper, to taste

Instructions:

Preparation:
- Preheat your oven to 450°F (230°C).
- In a small bowl, combine the minced garlic, chopped rosemary, chopped thyme, olive oil, salt, and pepper to make a paste.

Prepare the Prime Rib:
- Pat the prime rib roast dry with paper towels.
- Rub the garlic and herb paste all over the surface of the roast, ensuring it's evenly coated.

Roasting:
- Place the prime rib roast bone-side down on a roasting rack in a roasting pan.
- Roast the prime rib at 450°F (230°C) for 20 minutes to sear the outside.

Lower Temperature and Roast:
- After the initial sear, reduce the oven temperature to 325°F (165°C).
- Continue roasting for about 2 to 2.5 hours (or until desired doneness is reached), basting occasionally with the drippings.

Checking Doneness:

- Use a meat thermometer inserted into the thickest part of the roast to check for doneness. For medium-rare, the internal temperature should be around 135-140°F (57-60°C).

Resting the Roast:
- Once done, remove the prime rib from the oven and transfer it to a cutting board. Tent loosely with foil and let it rest for at least 20-30 minutes before carving.

Making the Au Jus:
- While the roast is resting, prepare the au jus sauce.
- Place the roasting pan with the drippings on the stove over medium heat.
- Add beef broth and red wine (if using), stirring and scraping up any browned bits from the bottom of the pan.
- Simmer for a few minutes until the sauce is slightly reduced. Season with salt and pepper to taste.

Carving and Serving:
- Carve the prime rib into thick slices and serve with the warm au jus sauce on the side.

Enjoy your garlic and herb prime rib as a luxurious centerpiece for your holiday table!

Honey Glazed Ham

Ingredients:

- 1 fully cooked bone-in ham (7-9 pounds)
- 1 cup honey
- 1/2 cup brown sugar
- 1/4 cup Dijon mustard
- 1/4 cup apple cider vinegar
- 1/4 teaspoon ground cloves
- Whole cloves (optional, for decoration)

Instructions:

   Preparation:
   - Preheat your oven to 325°F (165°C).

   Score the Ham:
   - Place the ham on a cutting board and score the surface in a diamond pattern with a sharp knife, about 1/4 inch deep.

   Prepare the Glaze:
   - In a saucepan over medium heat, combine the honey, brown sugar, Dijon mustard, apple cider vinegar, and ground cloves.
   - Stirring constantly, heat the mixture until the sugar is dissolved and the glaze is well combined. Remove from heat.

   Glaze the Ham:
   - Place the scored ham in a roasting pan, flat side down.
   - Brush or pour about half of the glaze over the ham, making sure to get the glaze into the cuts.

   Bake the Ham:
   - Cover the ham loosely with foil and bake in the preheated oven for about 1 hour, basting with the remaining glaze every 20 minutes.

   Decorate with Cloves (Optional):
   - If desired, stud the surface of the ham with whole cloves at the intersection points of the diamond pattern.

   Finish Baking:
   - Remove the foil during the last 15-20 minutes of baking to allow the ham to caramelize and develop a nice crust.

   Check Doneness:

- The internal temperature of the ham should reach 140°F (60°C) when fully heated through.

Rest and Serve:
- Once done, remove the ham from the oven and let it rest for about 10-15 minutes before slicing.
- Slice the ham and serve warm. Drizzle any pan juices over the slices for extra flavor.

Enjoy your delicious honey glazed ham as a delightful addition to your holiday feast!

Herb-Roasted Leg of Lamb

Ingredients:

- 1 leg of lamb (about 5-6 pounds), bone-in or boneless
- 4 cloves garlic, minced
- 2 tablespoons fresh rosemary, chopped
- 2 tablespoons fresh thyme, chopped
- 2 tablespoons fresh parsley, chopped
- Zest of 1 lemon
- 1/4 cup olive oil
- Salt and black pepper, to taste

Instructions:

Preparation:
- Preheat your oven to 375°F (190°C).

Prepare the Herb Rub:
- In a small bowl, combine the minced garlic, chopped rosemary, thyme, parsley, lemon zest, olive oil, salt, and pepper to make a herb rub.

Prepare the Lamb:
- Pat the leg of lamb dry with paper towels.
- Using a sharp knife, make small incisions all over the surface of the lamb.

Rub the Herb Mixture:
- Rub the herb mixture all over the leg of lamb, making sure to get the mixture into the incisions.

Roasting:
- Place the leg of lamb on a rack in a roasting pan.
- Roast in the preheated oven for about 1.5 to 2 hours, or until the internal temperature reaches your desired level of doneness (for medium-rare, aim for 135°F / 57°C).

Basting (Optional):
- If desired, baste the lamb with pan juices every 30 minutes during cooking to keep it moist and flavorful.

Rest and Serve:
- Once done, remove the lamb from the oven and tent loosely with foil.
- Let the lamb rest for about 15-20 minutes before carving. This allows the juices to redistribute and the lamb to become more tender.

Carving and Serving:
- Carve the lamb into slices and arrange on a serving platter.
- Serve the herb-roasted leg of lamb with your favorite sides and garnish with additional fresh herbs, if desired.

Enjoy this flavorful and tender herb-roasted leg of lamb as a wonderful centerpiece for your holiday dinner!

Stuffed Cornish Hens

Ingredients:

- 4 Cornish hens
- Salt and pepper, to taste
- 2 tablespoons olive oil

For the Stuffing:

- 1 cup cooked wild rice
- 1 cup finely chopped mushrooms (such as cremini or button)
- 1/2 cup finely chopped onion
- 1/2 cup finely chopped celery
- 2 cloves garlic, minced
- 2 tablespoons chopped fresh parsley
- 1/2 teaspoon dried thyme
- Salt and pepper, to taste
- 2 tablespoons butter

For the Glaze (Optional):

- 1/4 cup honey
- 2 tablespoons soy sauce
- 1 tablespoon Dijon mustard
- 1 tablespoon balsamic vinegar

Instructions:

Preheat Oven:
- Preheat your oven to 375°F (190°C).

Prepare the Stuffing:
- In a skillet, melt the butter over medium heat.
- Add the chopped mushrooms, onion, celery, and garlic. Cook until softened, about 5-7 minutes.
- Stir in the cooked wild rice, chopped parsley, dried thyme, salt, and pepper. Remove from heat and set aside.

Prepare the Cornish Hens:
- Rinse the Cornish hens under cold water and pat them dry with paper towels.
- Season the cavity of each hen with salt and pepper.
- Stuff each hen with the prepared stuffing mixture. Secure the openings with kitchen twine or toothpicks.

Truss the Hens (Optional):
- Truss the legs of each hen with kitchen twine to help them cook evenly and retain their shape.

Roasting:
- Place the stuffed Cornish hens in a roasting pan.
- Rub the olive oil all over the hens and season the outside with salt and pepper.

Roast the Hens:
- Roast the hens in the preheated oven for about 45-60 minutes, or until the internal temperature reaches 165°F (74°C) when measured with a meat thermometer inserted into the thickest part of the thigh.

Optional Glaze:
- In a small bowl, whisk together the honey, soy sauce, Dijon mustard, and balsamic vinegar to make the glaze.
- Brush the glaze over the hens during the last 15-20 minutes of cooking, allowing the hens to develop a shiny and flavorful coating.

Rest and Serve:
- Once done, remove the hens from the oven and let them rest for about 10 minutes before serving.
- Serve the stuffed Cornish hens with any remaining glaze drizzled over the top and your favorite holiday side dishes.

Enjoy these delicious stuffed Cornish hens as an elegant and flavorful main course for your holiday feast!

Vegan Lentil Loaf

Ingredients:

- 1 cup dry brown or green lentils
- 2 1/2 cups vegetable broth or water
- 1 tablespoon olive oil
- 1 onion, finely chopped
- 2 garlic cloves, minced
- 1 carrot, grated
- 1 celery stalk, finely chopped
- 1 red bell pepper, finely chopped
- 1 cup breadcrumbs (gluten-free if needed)
- 1/4 cup ground flaxseed meal
- 3 tablespoons tomato paste
- 2 tablespoons soy sauce or tamari
- 1 teaspoon dried thyme
- 1 teaspoon dried oregano
- Salt and pepper, to taste

Glaze:

- 1/4 cup ketchup
- 2 tablespoons maple syrup or agave syrup
- 1 tablespoon balsamic vinegar or apple cider vinegar

Instructions:

Cook Lentils: Rinse the lentils and place them in a saucepan with the vegetable broth or water. Bring to a boil, then reduce heat to a simmer. Cook for 20-25 minutes or until the lentils are tender and the liquid is absorbed. Drain any excess liquid and set aside.

Preheat Oven: Preheat your oven to 375°F (190°C) and lightly grease a loaf pan with oil.

Sauté Vegetables: In a skillet, heat olive oil over medium heat. Add the chopped onion and garlic, sautéing until translucent (about 3-4 minutes). Add grated carrot, celery, and bell pepper. Cook for an additional 5 minutes until vegetables are tender. Remove from heat and set aside.

Combine Ingredients: In a large mixing bowl, combine cooked lentils, sautéed vegetables, breadcrumbs, flaxseed meal, tomato paste, soy sauce, dried thyme, dried oregano, salt, and pepper. Mix well to combine all ingredients evenly.

Form the Loaf: Transfer the lentil mixture into the prepared loaf pan, pressing it down firmly and smoothing the top.

Make the Glaze: In a small bowl, whisk together the ketchup, maple syrup (or agave syrup), and balsamic vinegar (or apple cider vinegar). Spread this glaze evenly over the top of the lentil loaf.

Bake: Place the loaf pan in the preheated oven and bake for 40-45 minutes, or until the loaf is firm and the top is golden brown.

Cool and Serve: Allow the lentil loaf to cool in the pan for about 10 minutes before slicing. Serve slices of lentil loaf with your favorite sides like mashed potatoes, steamed vegetables, or a fresh salad.

This vegan lentil loaf is hearty, flavorful, and makes a perfect centerpiece for a plant-based meal. Enjoy!

Mushroom Wellington

Ingredients:

- 1 lb (450g) mixed mushrooms (such as button, cremini, or portobello), finely chopped
- 2 tablespoons olive oil
- 1 onion, finely chopped
- 3 garlic cloves, minced
- 1 teaspoon fresh thyme leaves (or 1/2 teaspoon dried thyme)
- Salt and pepper, to taste
- 1/4 cup white wine (optional)
- 1/2 cup breadcrumbs
- 1/4 cup chopped fresh parsley
- 1 sheet vegan puff pastry, thawed if frozen
- Vegan egg wash (1 tablespoon almond milk or soy milk mixed with 1 tablespoon maple syrup or agave syrup)

Instructions:

Prepare Mushroom Filling:
- Heat olive oil in a large skillet over medium heat. Add the chopped onion and cook until softened, about 5 minutes.
- Add minced garlic and cook for another minute until fragrant.
- Add the chopped mushrooms, thyme, salt, and pepper. Cook for about 10-12 minutes until the mushrooms release their moisture and start to brown.
- If using white wine, pour it into the skillet and cook for 2-3 minutes until the wine evaporates. Remove from heat and let the mixture cool slightly.

Assemble the Wellington:
- Preheat your oven to 400°F (200°C) and line a baking sheet with parchment paper.
- On a lightly floured surface, roll out the puff pastry sheet into a rectangle, approximately 12x14 inches.
- Spread the breadcrumbs evenly over the puff pastry, leaving a border around the edges.
- Spoon the mushroom mixture onto the breadcrumbs and spread it out evenly, again leaving a border around the edges.
- Sprinkle chopped fresh parsley over the mushroom mixture.

Fold and Seal:

- Brush the edges of the puff pastry with a little water to help seal them.
- Carefully fold the longer sides of the pastry over the mushroom filling, then fold the shorter ends to seal the filling completely.
- Place the Wellington seam side down on the prepared baking sheet.

Bake:
- Brush the top of the Wellington with the vegan egg wash for a golden finish.
- Using a sharp knife, score the top of the pastry lightly in a crisscross pattern.
- Bake in the preheated oven for 25-30 minutes or until the pastry is golden brown and puffed up.
- Remove from the oven and let it rest for a few minutes before slicing.

Serve:
- Slice the Mushroom Wellington into thick portions and serve warm.
- You can accompany it with roasted vegetables, mashed potatoes, or a side salad.

Enjoy this Mushroom Wellington as a delightful centerpiece for a vegan feast! The combination of earthy mushrooms and flaky pastry is sure to impress.

Cranberry and Pecan Stuffed Acorn Squash

Ingredients:

- 2 medium-sized acorn squash
- 1 tablespoon olive oil
- Salt and pepper, to taste
- 1 cup quinoa, rinsed
- 2 cups vegetable broth or water
- 1/2 cup pecans, chopped
- 1/2 cup dried cranberries
- 1 small onion, finely chopped
- 2 cloves garlic, minced
- 1 teaspoon dried thyme
- 1/2 teaspoon ground cinnamon
- 1/4 teaspoon ground nutmeg
- 2 tablespoons maple syrup
- Fresh parsley or sage, chopped (for garnish)

Instructions:

Prepare the Acorn Squash:
- Preheat your oven to 400°F (200°C).
- Wash the acorn squash and carefully cut them in half lengthwise. Scoop out the seeds and stringy pulp from each half.
- Rub the inside of each squash half with olive oil and season with salt and pepper.
- Place the squash halves cut-side down on a baking sheet lined with parchment paper.
- Roast in the oven for about 30-35 minutes, or until the squash is tender when pierced with a fork. Remove from the oven and set aside.

Prepare the Quinoa Filling:
- While the squash is roasting, prepare the quinoa. In a saucepan, combine the rinsed quinoa and vegetable broth or water. Bring to a boil, then reduce heat to low, cover, and simmer for 15-20 minutes, or until the quinoa is cooked and fluffy. Remove from heat and set aside.

Make the Cranberry and Pecan Stuffing:
- In a skillet, heat a tablespoon of olive oil over medium heat. Add chopped onion and garlic, and sauté until translucent and fragrant.

- Add the chopped pecans, dried cranberries, dried thyme, ground cinnamon, and ground nutmeg to the skillet. Stir and cook for another 2-3 minutes until the pecans are lightly toasted and the cranberries are softened.
- Stir in the cooked quinoa and maple syrup. Mix everything together until well combined. Taste and adjust seasoning with salt and pepper if needed.

Assemble and Serve:
- Fill each roasted acorn squash half with the quinoa stuffing mixture, pressing gently to pack it in.
- Place the stuffed squash back in the oven for another 10-15 minutes to heat through.
- Remove from the oven and garnish with freshly chopped parsley or sage.

Serve Warm:
- Serve the cranberry and pecan stuffed acorn squash halves as a main dish or a side dish for a festive meal.
- Enjoy the delicious flavors of the sweet cranberries, crunchy pecans, and warm spices paired with the tender roasted acorn squash.

This dish is both visually appealing and full of autumn flavors. It's sure to impress your guests and delight your taste buds!

Grilled Salmon with Dill Sauce

Ingredients:

For the Grilled Salmon:

- 4 salmon fillets (about 6 ounces each), skin-on or skinless
- Salt and pepper, to taste
- Olive oil, for brushing

For the Dill Sauce:

- 1/2 cup vegan mayonnaise
- 2 tablespoons chopped fresh dill
- 1 tablespoon Dijon mustard
- 1 tablespoon lemon juice
- 1 garlic clove, minced
- Salt and pepper, to taste

Optional Garnish:

- Fresh dill sprigs
- Lemon wedges

Instructions:

Prepare the Dill Sauce:
- In a small bowl, combine the vegan mayonnaise, chopped fresh dill, Dijon mustard, lemon juice, minced garlic, salt, and pepper. Stir well until all ingredients are thoroughly mixed. Taste and adjust seasoning if needed. Cover the bowl and refrigerate the dill sauce until ready to serve.

Prepare the Grilled Salmon:
- Preheat your grill to medium-high heat.
- Pat the salmon fillets dry with paper towels and season both sides with salt and pepper.
- Brush the grill grates with a bit of olive oil to prevent sticking.
- Place the salmon fillets on the preheated grill, skin-side down if using skin-on fillets.
- Grill for about 4-5 minutes per side, or until the salmon is cooked to your desired doneness and has nice grill marks. If the salmon is skin-on, you can gently flip it using a spatula after grilling on the skin side.

- Remove the grilled salmon from the heat and let it rest for a few minutes.

Serve:
- Transfer the grilled salmon fillets to serving plates.
- Spoon a generous amount of the prepared dill sauce over each salmon fillet.
- Garnish with fresh dill sprigs and serve with lemon wedges on the side.
- Enjoy your delicious grilled salmon with dill sauce alongside your favorite sides, such as roasted vegetables, rice, or a crisp green salad.

Tips:

- If you prefer a creamy and smooth dill sauce, you can blend the ingredients in a food processor or blender until smooth.
- Make sure not to overcook the salmon to keep it tender and juicy. Salmon is done when it flakes easily with a fork and is opaque in the center.
- Feel free to adjust the amount of dill, lemon juice, or garlic in the sauce according to your taste preferences.

This grilled salmon with dill sauce is perfect for a special dinner or a family gathering. The combination of tender grilled salmon and flavorful dill sauce is sure to impress!

Classic Beef Brisket

Ingredients:

- 1 beef brisket (about 4-5 pounds), preferably with a layer of fat on one side
- 2 tablespoons olive oil
- Salt and pepper, to taste
- 1 large onion, sliced
- 4 cloves garlic, minced
- 2 cups beef broth
- 1 cup red wine (optional)
- 2 tablespoons Worcestershire sauce
- 2 tablespoons tomato paste
- 2 bay leaves
- 1 teaspoon dried thyme
- 1 teaspoon dried rosemary
- 1 teaspoon paprika
- 1/2 teaspoon ground mustard
- 1/4 cup brown sugar
- 2 tablespoons cornstarch (optional, for thickening)

Instructions:

Preheat the Oven:
- Preheat your oven to 300°F (150°C).

Prepare the Brisket:
- Pat the brisket dry with paper towels. Season all sides of the brisket generously with salt and pepper.
- In a large oven-safe pot or Dutch oven, heat the olive oil over medium-high heat. Add the brisket, fat-side down, and sear for about 4-5 minutes until browned. Flip and sear the other side for an additional 4-5 minutes. Remove the brisket from the pot and set aside.

Saute the Onions and Garlic:
- Add the sliced onions to the pot and sauté for about 5 minutes until softened and slightly caramelized. Add the minced garlic and cook for another minute until fragrant.

Prepare the Braising Liquid:
- Pour in the beef broth and red wine (if using), scraping up any browned bits from the bottom of the pot.

- Stir in Worcestershire sauce, tomato paste, bay leaves, dried thyme, dried rosemary, paprika, ground mustard, and brown sugar. Mix well to combine.

Braise the Brisket:
- Return the seared brisket to the pot, placing it fat-side up in the braising liquid.
- Cover the pot with a lid and transfer it to the preheated oven.
- Braise the brisket for about 3.5 to 4 hours, or until the meat is very tender and can be easily shredded with a fork.

Rest and Serve:
- Once the brisket is done, carefully remove it from the pot and transfer it to a cutting board. Let it rest for about 15 minutes before slicing.
- Meanwhile, strain the braising liquid through a fine mesh sieve to remove solids and skim off any excess fat.
- If desired, thicken the braising liquid by combining 2 tablespoons of cornstarch with 2 tablespoons of cold water. Stir this mixture into the strained liquid and simmer until thickened into a gravy-like consistency.
- Slice the brisket against the grain into thick slices and serve with the strained braising liquid as a sauce.

Serving Suggestions:

- Serve the classic beef brisket with mashed potatoes, roasted vegetables, or creamy coleslaw.
- Garnish with fresh herbs like parsley or thyme for a pop of color and freshness.

Enjoy this tender and flavorful classic beef brisket as a comforting and satisfying meal for any occasion! The slow-cooking process ensures a deliciously moist and tender meat that's perfect for sharing with family and friends.

Roasted Duck with Orange Sauce

Ingredients:

For the Roasted Duck:

- 1 whole duck (about 4-5 pounds)
- Salt and pepper, to taste
- 2 oranges, quartered
- 4 garlic cloves, smashed
- 4 sprigs of fresh thyme
- 2 tablespoons olive oil

For the Orange Sauce:

- Juice of 2 oranges (about 1 cup)
- Zest of 1 orange
- 1/2 cup chicken or vegetable broth
- 1/4 cup orange marmalade
- 2 tablespoons soy sauce or tamari
- 2 tablespoons rice vinegar or white wine vinegar
- 2 tablespoons brown sugar
- 1 tablespoon cornstarch
- Salt and pepper, to taste

Instructions:

Preheat the Oven:
- Preheat your oven to 375°F (190°C).

Prepare the Duck:
- Remove the giblets from the duck cavity (if included) and pat the duck dry with paper towels.
- Season the inside and outside of the duck generously with salt and pepper.
- Stuff the cavity of the duck with quartered oranges, smashed garlic cloves, and fresh thyme sprigs.

Truss the Duck:
- Use kitchen twine to truss the duck by tying the legs together and securing the wings close to the body. This helps the duck cook evenly.

Roast the Duck:
- Place the duck on a rack set inside a roasting pan, breast-side up.

- Rub the skin of the duck with olive oil to help it crisp up during roasting.
- Roast the duck in the preheated oven for about 1.5 to 2 hours, or until the skin is golden brown and crispy and the internal temperature reaches 165°F (74°C) in the thickest part of the thigh.

Make the Orange Sauce:

- While the duck is roasting, prepare the orange sauce.
- In a saucepan, combine orange juice, orange zest, chicken or vegetable broth, orange marmalade, soy sauce or tamari, rice vinegar or white wine vinegar, and brown sugar.
- Bring the mixture to a simmer over medium heat, stirring occasionally.

Thicken the Sauce:

- In a small bowl, mix cornstarch with a tablespoon of cold water to create a slurry.
- Gradually whisk the cornstarch slurry into the simmering sauce, stirring constantly until the sauce thickens.
- Season the sauce with salt and pepper to taste. Keep warm until ready to serve.

Serve the Duck:

- Once the duck is cooked, remove it from the oven and let it rest for about 10-15 minutes before carving.
- Carve the duck into slices or pieces and arrange on a serving platter.
- Drizzle the orange sauce over the roasted duck slices or serve the sauce on the side.

Serving Suggestions:

- Serve the roasted duck with orange sauce alongside steamed rice, roasted potatoes, or a green vegetable like asparagus or green beans.
- Garnish with fresh orange slices, thyme sprigs, or chopped parsley for a beautiful presentation.

Enjoy this flavorful and impressive roasted duck with orange sauce for a special occasion or holiday meal! The combination of tender duck meat and citrusy orange glaze is sure to delight your taste buds.

Herb-Crusted Pork Tenderloin

Ingredients:

- 1 pork tenderloin (about 1 to 1.5 pounds)
- Salt and pepper, to taste
- 2 tablespoons Dijon mustard
- 2 tablespoons olive oil

For the Herb Crust:

- 1 cup fresh breadcrumbs (from about 2 slices of bread)
- 2 cloves garlic, minced
- 2 tablespoons chopped fresh herbs (such as parsley, thyme, rosemary, or a combination)
- Zest of 1 lemon
- Salt and pepper, to taste
- 2 tablespoons olive oil

Instructions:

Preheat the Oven:
- Preheat your oven to 400°F (200°C).

Prepare the Pork Tenderloin:
- Pat the pork tenderloin dry with paper towels. Season generously with salt and pepper.
- In a small bowl, mix together the Dijon mustard and olive oil. Brush this mixture evenly over the surface of the pork tenderloin.

Make the Herb Crust:
- In a food processor, pulse the fresh breadcrumbs, minced garlic, chopped fresh herbs, lemon zest, salt, and pepper until combined.
- With the food processor running, slowly drizzle in the olive oil until the mixture resembles coarse crumbs. Alternatively, you can mix these ingredients by hand in a bowl.

Coat the Pork Tenderloin:
- Press the herb crust mixture onto the Dijon mustard-coated pork tenderloin, covering it evenly with the breadcrumb mixture.

Sear the Pork Tenderloin (Optional):
- Heat an oven-safe skillet or frying pan over medium-high heat. Add a bit of olive oil.

- Sear the pork tenderloin on all sides until golden brown, about 2-3 minutes per side. This step is optional but helps to develop a nice crust on the outside of the tenderloin.

Roast the Pork Tenderloin:
- Transfer the pork tenderloin (in the skillet if seared) to the preheated oven.
- Roast for about 15-20 minutes, or until the internal temperature of the pork reaches 145°F (63°C) for medium-rare or 160°F (71°C) for medium, using a meat thermometer inserted into the thickest part of the tenderloin.
- Remove the pork tenderloin from the oven and let it rest for 5-10 minutes before slicing.

Slice and Serve:
- Slice the herb-crusted pork tenderloin into thick slices.
- Serve immediately with your favorite sides such as roasted vegetables, mashed potatoes, or a fresh green salad.

Serving Suggestions:

- Garnish the sliced pork tenderloin with additional chopped fresh herbs for a pop of color and freshness.
- Drizzle with a squeeze of lemon juice or serve with a dollop of Dijon mustard on the side for extra flavor.

Enjoy this herb-crusted pork tenderloin as a flavorful and elegant main course that's sure to impress! The combination of juicy pork and herby crust makes it a delightful meal for any occasion.

Vegetarian Mushroom Gravy

Ingredients:

- 2 tablespoons butter or olive oil (for vegan option)
- 1 onion, finely chopped
- 2 garlic cloves, minced
- 8 ounces (about 225g) cremini mushrooms, sliced
- 2 tablespoons all-purpose flour (use gluten-free flour if needed)
- 2 cups vegetable broth
- 1 tablespoon soy sauce or tamari
- 1 teaspoon dried thyme
- Salt and pepper, to taste
- 1-2 tablespoons chopped fresh parsley (optional, for garnish)

Instructions:

Saute the Onions and Garlic:
- In a skillet or saucepan, heat the butter or olive oil over medium heat.
- Add the chopped onion and sauté for 3-4 minutes until translucent.
- Add the minced garlic and sliced mushrooms to the skillet. Cook for another 5-6 minutes, stirring occasionally, until the mushrooms are tender and browned.

Make the Gravy:
- Sprinkle the flour over the mushroom mixture in the skillet. Stir well to coat the mushrooms and cook for 1-2 minutes to lightly toast the flour.
- Gradually pour in the vegetable broth while stirring continuously to prevent lumps from forming.
- Add the soy sauce or tamari, dried thyme, salt, and pepper. Stir to combine.

Simmer and Thicken:
- Bring the gravy to a simmer, then reduce the heat to low.
- Let the gravy simmer gently for 5-7 minutes, stirring occasionally, until it thickens to your desired consistency. If the gravy becomes too thick, you can add more vegetable broth to thin it out.

Adjust Seasoning:
- Taste the gravy and adjust the seasoning with salt and pepper as needed. You can also add more soy sauce or tamari for extra umami flavor.

Serve:
- Once the gravy has reached the desired thickness, remove it from the heat.

- Serve the vegetarian mushroom gravy hot, ladled over mashed potatoes, roasted vegetables, or your favorite vegetarian dishes.
- Garnish with chopped fresh parsley if desired.

Tips:

- For a richer flavor, you can use a combination of different mushroom varieties such as shiitake or portobello along with cremini mushrooms.
- If you prefer a smoother gravy, you can blend the mixture using an immersion blender or transfer it to a blender (after cooling slightly) and blend until smooth.
- Leftover mushroom gravy can be stored in an airtight container in the refrigerator for up to 3-4 days. Reheat gently on the stovetop or in the microwave before serving.

This vegetarian mushroom gravy is a comforting and versatile addition to any meal. Enjoy its savory goodness with your favorite vegetarian dishes!

Creamy Butternut Squash Soup

Ingredients:

- 1 large butternut squash (about 3 pounds), peeled, seeded, and cut into 1-inch cubes
- 2 tablespoons olive oil
- Salt and pepper, to taste
- 1 onion, chopped
- 2 cloves garlic, minced
- 1-inch piece of ginger, peeled and minced
- 4 cups vegetable broth
- 1 (13.5 oz) can coconut milk (full-fat for creaminess)
- 1 teaspoon curry powder (optional)
- 1/2 teaspoon ground cinnamon
- 1/4 teaspoon ground nutmeg
- Juice of 1/2 lemon
- Fresh cilantro or parsley, chopped (for garnish)

Instructions:

Roast the Butternut Squash:
- Preheat your oven to 400°F (200°C).
- Place the cubed butternut squash on a baking sheet. Drizzle with olive oil, season with salt and pepper, and toss to coat evenly.
- Roast the squash in the preheated oven for 25-30 minutes, or until tender and caramelized. Remove from the oven and set aside.

Saute the Aromatics:
- In a large pot or Dutch oven, heat 1 tablespoon of olive oil over medium heat.
- Add the chopped onion, minced garlic, and minced ginger. Saute for 3-4 minutes until the onion is translucent and fragrant.

Simmer the Soup:
- Add the roasted butternut squash to the pot with the sautéed aromatics.
- Pour in the vegetable broth and bring the mixture to a simmer.
- Stir in the coconut milk, curry powder (if using), ground cinnamon, and ground nutmeg.
- Simmer the soup, uncovered, for about 15-20 minutes to allow the flavors to meld together.

Blend the Soup:

- Remove the pot from the heat. Use an immersion blender to puree the soup until smooth and creamy. Alternatively, carefully transfer the soup in batches to a blender and blend until smooth.
- If the soup is too thick, you can add more vegetable broth or water to reach your desired consistency.

Season and Serve:
- Stir in the lemon juice to brighten the flavors of the soup.
- Taste and adjust seasoning with salt and pepper as needed.
- Ladle the creamy butternut squash soup into bowls.
- Garnish each serving with chopped fresh cilantro or parsley.

Serving Suggestions:

- Serve the creamy butternut squash soup with crusty bread or garlic bread for dipping.
- Add a dollop of coconut cream or Greek yogurt on top for extra creaminess.
- Enjoy this soup as a comforting starter or light meal on its own.

This creamy butternut squash soup is vegan-friendly, gluten-free, and bursting with autumn flavors. It's sure to become a favorite cold-weather recipe in your household!

Shrimp Scampi

Ingredients:

- 1 pound (450g) large shrimp, peeled and deveined
- Salt and pepper, to taste
- 4 tablespoons unsalted butter
- 2 tablespoons olive oil
- 4 cloves garlic, minced
- 1/4 teaspoon red pepper flakes (adjust to taste)
- 1/4 cup dry white wine (such as Sauvignon Blanc or Pinot Grigio)
- Juice of 1 lemon
- Zest of 1 lemon
- 1/4 cup chopped fresh parsley
- 12 ounces (340g) linguine or spaghetti
- Grated Parmesan cheese, for serving (optional)

Instructions:

Prepare the Shrimp:
- Pat the shrimp dry with paper towels and season with salt and pepper.

Cook the Pasta:
- Bring a large pot of salted water to a boil.
- Cook the linguine or spaghetti according to the package instructions until al dente. Reserve about 1 cup of pasta cooking water before draining.

Make the Shrimp Scampi:
- In a large skillet, heat 2 tablespoons of butter and 1 tablespoon of olive oil over medium-high heat.
- Add the minced garlic and red pepper flakes to the skillet. Cook for about 1 minute until the garlic is fragrant but not browned.
- Add the shrimp to the skillet in a single layer. Cook for 1-2 minutes per side until the shrimp turns pink and opaque. Remove the shrimp from the skillet and set aside.

Prepare the Sauce:
- Deglaze the skillet with white wine, scraping up any browned bits from the bottom of the pan.
- Add the remaining 2 tablespoons of butter to the skillet. Allow it to melt and combine with the wine.
- Stir in the lemon juice and lemon zest. Cook for another minute to let the flavors meld together.

- Return the cooked shrimp to the skillet. Add chopped parsley and toss everything together to coat the shrimp with the sauce. Season with additional salt and pepper if needed.

Combine with Pasta:
- Add the drained linguine or spaghetti to the skillet with the shrimp and sauce.
- Toss everything together, adding a splash of reserved pasta cooking water as needed to loosen the sauce and coat the pasta evenly.

Serve:
- Divide the shrimp scampi pasta among serving plates or bowls.
- Garnish with additional chopped parsley and grated Parmesan cheese if desired.
- Serve immediately with crusty bread on the side.

Tips:

- For extra flavor, you can add a splash of seafood broth or chicken broth along with the white wine.
- Feel free to adjust the amount of garlic and red pepper flakes to suit your taste preferences.
- Serve shrimp scampi with a side of steamed vegetables or a fresh green salad for a complete meal.

Enjoy this homemade shrimp scampi with its buttery garlic sauce and bright lemony flavors. It's a delightful and satisfying dish that's perfect for weeknight dinners or special occasions!

Lemon Herb Roasted Chicken

Ingredients:

- 1 whole chicken (about 4-5 pounds), giblets removed
- Salt and pepper, to taste
- 1 lemon, halved
- 4 garlic cloves, minced
- 2 tablespoons chopped fresh herbs (such as rosemary, thyme, and parsley)
- 3 tablespoons olive oil
- 1 tablespoon Dijon mustard
- 1 tablespoon honey or maple syrup (optional, for a touch of sweetness)

Instructions:

Preheat the Oven:
- Preheat your oven to 425°F (220°C).

Prepare the Chicken:
- Pat the chicken dry with paper towels. Season the inside and outside of the chicken generously with salt and pepper.
- Stuff the cavity of the chicken with lemon halves, minced garlic, and chopped fresh herbs.

Truss the Chicken (Optional):
- Trussing the chicken helps it cook more evenly and keeps the shape compact. Use kitchen twine to tie the legs together and tuck the wing tips under the body.

Make the Herb Paste:
- In a small bowl, mix together olive oil, Dijon mustard, and honey or maple syrup (if using) to create a paste.
- Rub the herb paste all over the surface of the chicken, making sure to coat it evenly.

Roast the Chicken:
- Place the seasoned chicken on a roasting rack set inside a roasting pan, breast-side up.
- Roast the chicken in the preheated oven for about 1 to 1.5 hours, or until the internal temperature reaches 165°F (74°C) when measured with a meat thermometer inserted into the thickest part of the thigh.
- Baste the chicken with pan juices halfway through the cooking time to keep it moist and flavorful.

Rest and Serve:

- Once the chicken is cooked through and the skin is golden brown and crispy, remove it from the oven.
- Tent the chicken loosely with foil and let it rest for about 10-15 minutes before carving. This allows the juices to redistribute and the chicken to become more tender.

Carve and Garnish:
- Carve the roasted chicken into serving pieces.
- Serve the lemon herb roasted chicken with pan juices spooned over the top.
- Garnish with additional chopped fresh herbs if desired.

Serving Suggestions:

- Serve the lemon herb roasted chicken with roasted vegetables such as potatoes, carrots, and Brussels sprouts.
- Pair it with a side salad or steamed greens for a complete meal.
- Enjoy the leftovers in sandwiches, salads, or pasta dishes.

This lemon herb roasted chicken is a timeless dish that's sure to be a hit at the dinner table. The combination of herbs, garlic, and lemon infuses the chicken with delicious flavors and aroma. Enjoy!

Garlic Mashed Potatoes

Ingredients:

- 2 pounds (about 900g) Yukon Gold or Russet potatoes, peeled and cut into chunks
- Salt, for cooking potatoes
- 4 cloves garlic, peeled
- 1/2 cup (1 stick) unsalted butter, cut into pieces
- 1/2 cup milk or cream (adjust amount based on desired creaminess)
- Salt and pepper, to taste
- Chopped fresh chives or parsley, for garnish (optional)

Instructions:

Boil the Potatoes:
- Place the potato chunks and whole garlic cloves in a large pot. Cover with cold water and add a generous pinch of salt.
- Bring the water to a boil over high heat, then reduce the heat to medium-low and simmer for 15-20 minutes or until the potatoes are fork-tender.

Drain and Mash:
- Drain the cooked potatoes and garlic cloves thoroughly in a colander.
- Return the drained potatoes and garlic to the pot.

Make the Garlic Butter:
- While the potatoes are still hot, add the butter pieces to the pot.
- Allow the butter to melt from the residual heat of the potatoes and garlic.

Mash the Potatoes:
- Use a potato masher or a fork to mash the potatoes and garlic until smooth. Alternatively, you can use a potato ricer for an extra silky texture.
- Gradually pour in the milk or cream while mashing, until the potatoes reach your desired consistency. Add more milk or cream as needed.
- Season the mashed potatoes with salt and pepper to taste. Be sure to taste and adjust seasoning as necessary.

Serve:
- Transfer the garlic mashed potatoes to a serving bowl.
- Garnish with chopped fresh chives or parsley if desired.
- Serve the mashed potatoes hot alongside your favorite main dishes.

Tips:

- To infuse more garlic flavor into the mashed potatoes, you can simmer the peeled garlic cloves in the milk or cream (heated separately) before adding it to the potatoes.
- For extra creaminess, you can substitute some or all of the milk with heavy cream or sour cream.
- Feel free to customize the mashed potatoes by adding grated Parmesan cheese, roasted garlic, or a touch of horseradish for extra flavor.

These creamy and flavorful garlic mashed potatoes are a perfect side dish for any meal.

They're easy to make and always a crowd-pleaser. Enjoy!

Sweet Potato Casserole with Pecan Streusel

Ingredients:

For the Sweet Potato Base:

- 4-5 medium sweet potatoes (about 3 pounds), peeled and cubed
- 1/2 cup unsalted butter, melted
- 1/4 cup brown sugar
- 1/4 cup maple syrup or honey
- 1 teaspoon vanilla extract
- 1/2 teaspoon ground cinnamon
- 1/4 teaspoon ground nutmeg
- 1/2 cup milk (dairy or non-dairy)
- 2 large eggs, lightly beaten
- Salt, to taste

For the Pecan Streusel Topping:

- 1 cup chopped pecans
- 1/2 cup all-purpose flour (or almond flour for gluten-free option)
- 1/2 cup brown sugar
- 1/4 cup unsalted butter, melted
- 1/2 teaspoon ground cinnamon
- Pinch of salt

Instructions:

Cook the Sweet Potatoes:
- Place the cubed sweet potatoes in a large pot and cover with water.
- Bring to a boil over high heat, then reduce the heat to medium-low and simmer for 15-20 minutes, or until the sweet potatoes are tender when pierced with a fork.
- Drain the cooked sweet potatoes and set aside.

Preheat the Oven:
- Preheat your oven to 350°F (175°C). Lightly grease a 9x13-inch baking dish.

Prepare the Sweet Potato Base:
- In a large mixing bowl, mash the cooked sweet potatoes until smooth.

- Add melted butter, brown sugar, maple syrup or honey, vanilla extract, ground cinnamon, ground nutmeg, milk, beaten eggs, and salt. Mix until well combined and smooth.

Transfer to Baking Dish:
- Spread the sweet potato mixture evenly in the prepared baking dish, smoothing the top with a spatula.

Make the Pecan Streusel Topping:
- In a separate bowl, combine chopped pecans, flour, brown sugar, melted butter, ground cinnamon, and a pinch of salt. Mix until the mixture resembles coarse crumbs.

Add the Streusel Topping:
- Sprinkle the pecan streusel topping evenly over the sweet potato mixture in the baking dish.

Bake the Casserole:
- Place the baking dish in the preheated oven and bake for 25-30 minutes, or until the sweet potato base is heated through and the pecan streusel topping is golden brown and crispy.

Serve:
- Remove the sweet potato casserole from the oven and let it cool slightly before serving.
- Serve warm as a side dish for holiday meals or special occasions.

Tips:

- You can prepare the sweet potato casserole ahead of time and refrigerate it (covered) before baking. Simply let it come to room temperature before baking as directed.
- If the pecan streusel topping browns too quickly during baking, cover the casserole loosely with aluminum foil to prevent over-browning.
- Feel free to adjust the sweetness of the casserole by adding more or less brown sugar and maple syrup/honey to suit your taste preferences.

This sweet potato casserole with pecan streusel is a delightful combination of creamy, sweet, and crunchy textures. It's sure to be a hit at your next gathering!

Green Bean Almondine

Ingredients:

- 1 pound (450g) fresh green beans, trimmed
- Salt, for blanching and seasoning
- 2 tablespoons unsalted butter
- 1/3 cup sliced almonds
- 1-2 cloves garlic, minced (optional)
- Zest of 1 lemon
- 2 tablespoons fresh lemon juice
- Salt and pepper, to taste

Instructions:

Blanch the Green Beans:
- Bring a large pot of salted water to a boil. Add the green beans and cook for 3-4 minutes, or until the beans are bright green and crisp-tender.
- Immediately transfer the green beans to a bowl of ice water to stop the cooking process. Drain and set aside.

Toast the Almonds:
- In a large skillet, melt the butter over medium heat.
- Add the sliced almonds to the skillet and toast them for 2-3 minutes, stirring frequently, until the almonds are golden and fragrant. Be careful not to burn them.
- If using minced garlic, add it to the skillet with the almonds and cook for an additional 30 seconds until fragrant.

Finish the Dish:
- Add the blanched green beans to the skillet with the toasted almonds and garlic.
- Toss everything together gently to coat the green beans with the buttery almond mixture.
- Add lemon zest and lemon juice to the skillet. Continue to toss until the green beans are heated through and well coated with the lemony butter sauce.
- Season with salt and pepper to taste.

Serve:
- Transfer the green beans almondine to a serving dish.
- Garnish with additional lemon zest or sliced almonds if desired.
- Serve immediately as a delicious side dish.

Tips:

- You can blanch the green beans ahead of time and keep them refrigerated until you're ready to finish the dish.
- Feel free to customize the dish by adding chopped fresh herbs such as parsley or thyme for extra flavor.
- For a richer sauce, you can add a splash of white wine or chicken broth to the skillet along with the lemon juice.

Green beans almondine is a versatile and elegant side dish that pairs beautifully with roasted meats, poultry, or seafood. It's perfect for holiday dinners, special occasions, or everyday meals. Enjoy this delicious and nutritious dish!

Roasted Brussels Sprouts with Balsamic Glaze

Ingredients:

- 1.5 pounds (680g) Brussels sprouts, trimmed and halved
- 2 tablespoons olive oil
- Salt and pepper, to taste
- 1/4 cup balsamic vinegar
- 1 tablespoon honey or maple syrup (optional, for sweetness)
- 1-2 cloves garlic, minced (optional)
- Freshly grated Parmesan cheese, for garnish (optional)

Instructions:

Preheat the Oven:
- Preheat your oven to 400°F (200°C).

Prepare the Brussels Sprouts:
- Trim the ends off the Brussels sprouts and cut them in half lengthwise.
- Place the halved Brussels sprouts on a large baking sheet.

Roast the Brussels Sprouts:
- Drizzle the Brussels sprouts with olive oil and season with salt and pepper.
- Toss the Brussels sprouts to coat them evenly with the oil and seasoning.
- Spread the Brussels sprouts out in a single layer on the baking sheet.
- Roast in the preheated oven for 20-25 minutes, or until the Brussels sprouts are tender and caramelized, tossing halfway through cooking for even browning.

Make the Balsamic Glaze:
- While the Brussels sprouts are roasting, prepare the balsamic glaze.
- In a small saucepan, combine the balsamic vinegar and honey or maple syrup (if using).
- Add minced garlic to the saucepan if desired for extra flavor.
- Bring the mixture to a simmer over medium heat. Cook for 8-10 minutes, stirring occasionally, until the glaze thickens and reduces by half. It should coat the back of a spoon.

Combine and Serve:
- Once the Brussels sprouts are roasted to perfection, transfer them to a serving dish.
- Drizzle the balsamic glaze over the roasted Brussels sprouts.
- Toss gently to coat the Brussels sprouts with the glaze.
- If desired, garnish with freshly grated Parmesan cheese for extra flavor.

Serve Immediately:
- Serve the roasted Brussels sprouts with balsamic glaze hot as a delicious side dish.

Tips:

- Customize the dish by adding crispy cooked bacon or toasted nuts (such as walnuts or pecans) to the roasted Brussels sprouts before drizzling with balsamic glaze.
- For a vegan version, omit the Parmesan cheese or use a dairy-free alternative.
- Make sure to keep an eye on the balsamic glaze while cooking to prevent it from burning. It should thicken and become syrupy.

Roasted Brussels sprouts with balsamic glaze make a wonderful addition to any meal, from weeknight dinners to holiday feasts. Enjoy the combination of caramelized Brussels sprouts with the sweet and tangy balsamic reduction!

Cranberry Orange Relish

Ingredients:

- 12 ounces (340g) fresh cranberries
- 1 large orange, zest and juice
- 1/2 cup granulated sugar (adjust to taste)
- 1/4 cup water
- 1 cinnamon stick (optional)
- Pinch of salt

Instructions:

Prepare the Cranberries:
- Rinse the fresh cranberries under cold water and discard any damaged or bruised ones.

Zest and Juice the Orange:
- Use a microplane or fine grater to zest the entire orange.
- Cut the orange in half and juice it to yield about 1/4 cup of fresh orange juice.

Cook the Relish:
- In a medium saucepan, combine the cranberries, orange zest, orange juice, granulated sugar, water, cinnamon stick (if using), and a pinch of salt.
- Bring the mixture to a boil over medium-high heat, stirring occasionally.

Simmer and Thicken:
- Once the mixture comes to a boil, reduce the heat to medium-low and let it simmer for 10-15 minutes, or until the cranberries burst and the mixture thickens to a relish-like consistency.
- Stir occasionally to prevent sticking and burning.

Adjust Sweetness:
- Taste the cranberry orange relish and adjust the sweetness by adding more sugar if desired. Keep in mind that the relish will continue to sweeten as it cools.

Cool and Serve:
- Remove the cinnamon stick from the relish (if used) and let the relish cool to room temperature.
- Transfer the cranberry orange relish to a serving bowl or jar.
- Refrigerate until ready to serve.

Serve:

- Serve the cranberry orange relish as a condiment alongside roasted turkey, chicken, pork, or any holiday meal.
- You can also use the relish as a spread on toast, biscuits, or sandwiches.

Tips:

- For a spicier twist, add a pinch of ground cinnamon, ground cloves, or a dash of cayenne pepper to the relish.
- Customize the relish by adding finely chopped nuts (such as pecans or walnuts) for extra texture and flavor.
- This cranberry orange relish can be made ahead of time and stored in the refrigerator for up to 1 week.

Enjoy this homemade cranberry orange relish with its delightful blend of tart cranberries and citrusy orange flavor. It's a festive and versatile condiment that will elevate your holiday meals!

Classic Bread Stuffing

Ingredients:

- 1 loaf of day-old French bread or sourdough bread (about 1 pound), cut into 1-inch cubes (about 10 cups)
- 1/2 cup (1 stick) unsalted butter, plus extra for greasing the baking dish
- 1 large onion, diced
- 2-3 stalks celery, diced
- 2-3 cloves garlic, minced
- 2-3 teaspoons chopped fresh sage (or 1 teaspoon dried sage)
- 2-3 teaspoons chopped fresh thyme (or 1 teaspoon dried thyme)
- Salt and pepper, to taste
- 2-3 cups low-sodium chicken or vegetable broth
- 2 large eggs, beaten (optional, for a richer stuffing)

Instructions:

Prepare the Bread Cubes:
- Preheat your oven to 300°F (150°C).
- Spread the bread cubes in a single layer on a baking sheet.
- Bake the bread cubes in the preheated oven for 15-20 minutes, or until they are dry and slightly toasted. This step helps the bread cubes hold their shape in the stuffing.

Saute the Vegetables:
- In a large skillet or frying pan, melt the butter over medium heat.
- Add the diced onion and celery to the skillet. Cook for 5-7 minutes, or until the vegetables are softened and translucent.
- Add the minced garlic, chopped sage, and thyme to the skillet. Cook for an additional 1-2 minutes until fragrant. Season with salt and pepper to taste.

Combine Ingredients:
- In a large mixing bowl, combine the toasted bread cubes with the sautéed vegetables and herbs.
- Pour 2 cups of chicken or vegetable broth over the mixture, tossing gently to moisten the bread cubes. Add more broth as needed until the bread cubes are evenly moistened but not soggy.
- If using, stir in the beaten eggs to bind the stuffing together.

Bake the Stuffing:
- Preheat your oven to 350°F (175°C).

- Transfer the stuffing mixture to a greased 9x13-inch baking dish or a large oven-safe skillet.
- Cover the dish with aluminum foil and bake in the preheated oven for 30 minutes.
- Remove the foil and continue baking for an additional 15-20 minutes, or until the top is golden brown and crispy.

Serve:
- Remove the stuffing from the oven and let it rest for a few minutes before serving.
- Serve the classic bread stuffing warm as a delicious side dish for Thanksgiving, Christmas, or any festive meal.

Tips:

- Customize the stuffing by adding chopped apples, dried cranberries, toasted nuts (such as pecans or walnuts), or cooked crumbled sausage for extra flavor and texture.
- Make the stuffing vegetarian by using vegetable broth instead of chicken broth.
- Leftover stuffing can be stored in an airtight container in the refrigerator for up to 3-4 days. Reheat in the oven or microwave before serving.

Enjoy this classic bread stuffing as a comforting and flavorful addition to your holiday table or family dinners!

Wild Rice Pilaf

Ingredients:

- 1 cup wild rice
- 1 tablespoon olive oil or butter
- 1 onion, finely chopped
- 2 cloves garlic, minced
- 2 celery stalks, finely chopped
- 1 carrot, finely chopped
- 1/2 cup sliced mushrooms (optional)
- 2 cups vegetable or chicken broth
- 1/2 teaspoon dried thyme
- 1/2 teaspoon dried sage
- Salt and pepper, to taste
- 1/4 cup chopped fresh parsley (optional, for garnish)
- 1/4 cup chopped toasted nuts (such as almonds or pecans) (optional)
- 1/4 cup dried cranberries or chopped apricots (optional)

Instructions:

Rinse and Cook the Wild Rice:
- Rinse the wild rice under cold water.
- In a medium saucepan, combine the wild rice with 2 cups of water. Bring to a boil over high heat.
- Reduce the heat to low, cover, and simmer for 40-45 minutes, or until the wild rice is tender and has split open. Drain any excess water and set aside.

Saute the Vegetables:
- In a large skillet or sauté pan, heat the olive oil or butter over medium heat.
- Add the chopped onion, garlic, celery, carrot, and mushrooms (if using) to the skillet. Cook for 5-7 minutes, or until the vegetables are softened.

Combine and Season:
- Add the cooked wild rice to the skillet with the sautéed vegetables.
- Pour in the vegetable or chicken broth and add the dried thyme, dried sage, salt, and pepper. Stir well to combine.

Simmer the Pilaf:
- Bring the mixture to a simmer. Reduce the heat to low, cover, and let it simmer for 15-20 minutes, or until most of the liquid is absorbed and the wild rice is fully cooked.

Add Optional Ingredients:
- Stir in the chopped fresh parsley, toasted nuts (such as almonds or pecans), and dried cranberries or chopped apricots (if using). These optional ingredients add texture and flavor to the pilaf.

Serve:
- Transfer the wild rice pilaf to a serving dish.
- Garnish with additional chopped parsley if desired.
- Serve the pilaf warm as a delicious side dish or vegetarian main course.

Tips:

- Wild rice can sometimes take longer to cook depending on the variety. Follow the package instructions for cooking times and water ratios.
- Feel free to customize the wild rice pilaf by adding other vegetables such as bell peppers, peas, or spinach.
- For a richer flavor, substitute some of the broth with white wine or add a splash of lemon juice before serving.

This wild rice pilaf is a versatile and satisfying dish that pairs well with roasted poultry, grilled fish, or as a hearty vegetarian meal on its own. Enjoy the earthy flavors and wholesome goodness of this delicious wild rice pilaf!

Pumpkin Risotto

Ingredients:

- 1 cup Arborio rice
- 4 cups vegetable or chicken broth
- 1 cup pumpkin puree (canned or homemade)
- 1 small onion, finely chopped
- 2 cloves garlic, minced
- 1/2 cup dry white wine (optional)
- 2 tablespoons butter
- 1 tablespoon olive oil
- 1/2 cup grated Parmesan cheese
- 1/2 teaspoon dried sage
- 1/4 teaspoon ground nutmeg
- Salt and pepper, to taste
- Fresh parsley or sage, chopped (for garnish)

Instructions:

Prepare the Broth:
- In a saucepan, heat the vegetable or chicken broth over low heat. Keep it warm but not boiling.

Saute the Onion and Garlic:
- In a large skillet or saucepan, heat the olive oil and 1 tablespoon of butter over medium heat.
- Add the chopped onion and sauté for 2-3 minutes until translucent.
- Add the minced garlic and continue to cook for another 1-2 minutes until fragrant.

Toast the Rice:
- Add the Arborio rice to the skillet with the onions and garlic. Stir to coat the rice with the oil and butter.
- Toast the rice for 1-2 minutes until the edges become translucent.

Deglaze with Wine (Optional):
- Pour in the white wine (if using) and stir continuously until the wine is absorbed by the rice.

Add Pumpkin and Seasonings:
- Stir in the pumpkin puree, dried sage, and ground nutmeg.
- Season with salt and pepper to taste.

Cook the Risotto:

- Begin adding the warm broth to the rice mixture, one ladleful at a time.
- Stir the rice constantly and allow each addition of broth to be absorbed before adding more.
- Continue this process for about 18-20 minutes or until the rice is creamy and tender but still slightly firm (al dente).

Finish the Risotto:
- Stir in the remaining tablespoon of butter and grated Parmesan cheese.
- Taste and adjust seasoning if needed.

Serve:
- Transfer the pumpkin risotto to serving plates or bowls.
- Garnish with chopped fresh parsley or sage.
- Serve immediately while hot.

Tips:

- If you prefer a richer flavor, you can substitute some of the broth with heavy cream or half-and-half.
- Feel free to add additional ingredients such as cooked bacon, roasted butternut squash cubes, or toasted pine nuts for extra flavor and texture.
- Leftover pumpkin risotto can be stored in an airtight container in the refrigerator for up to 3 days. Reheat gently on the stovetop with a splash of broth or water to loosen the consistency.

Enjoy this creamy and flavorful pumpkin risotto as a delightful main course or side dish during the fall season. It's a wonderful way to celebrate the harvest and savor the flavors of pumpkin!

Garlic Parmesan Roasted Asparagus

Ingredients:

- 1 pound (450g) fresh asparagus spears, tough ends trimmed
- 2 tablespoons olive oil
- 2-3 cloves garlic, minced
- Salt and pepper, to taste
- 1/4 cup grated Parmesan cheese
- Lemon wedges, for serving (optional)
- Chopped fresh parsley, for garnish (optional)

Instructions:

Preheat the Oven:
- Preheat your oven to 425°F (220°C). Line a baking sheet with parchment paper or foil for easy cleanup.

Prepare the Asparagus:
- Rinse the asparagus spears under cold water and pat them dry with paper towels.
- Trim the tough ends off the asparagus spears (usually about 1-2 inches from the bottom).

Season the Asparagus:
- Place the trimmed asparagus spears on the prepared baking sheet.
- Drizzle olive oil over the asparagus and sprinkle minced garlic, salt, and pepper evenly over the spears.
- Toss the asparagus gently to coat them evenly with the oil, garlic, salt, and pepper.

Roast the Asparagus:
- Arrange the seasoned asparagus spears in a single layer on the baking sheet.
- Roast in the preheated oven for 12-15 minutes, or until the asparagus is tender and slightly caramelized, tossing halfway through cooking for even roasting.

Add Parmesan Cheese:
- Remove the baking sheet from the oven and sprinkle grated Parmesan cheese over the roasted asparagus.
- Return the baking sheet to the oven and roast for an additional 2-3 minutes, or until the cheese is melted and golden.

Serve:

- Transfer the garlic Parmesan roasted asparagus to a serving platter.
- Garnish with chopped fresh parsley if desired.
- Serve hot with lemon wedges on the side for squeezing over the asparagus just before eating.

Tips:

- Choose asparagus spears that are uniform in size for even cooking.
- Feel free to adjust the amount of garlic, Parmesan cheese, salt, and pepper according to your taste preferences.
- For a variation, you can add a sprinkle of red pepper flakes or lemon zest to the roasted asparagus for extra flavor.

This garlic Parmesan roasted asparagus makes a delightful side dish that complements any meal. It's quick to prepare and bursting with flavor. Enjoy the tender-crisp asparagus spears with the savory Parmesan cheese and aromatic garlic!

Creamed Spinach

Ingredients:

- 1 pound (450g) fresh spinach leaves, washed and trimmed
- 2 tablespoons unsalted butter
- 2 cloves garlic, minced
- 2 tablespoons all-purpose flour
- 1 cup whole milk or heavy cream
- 1/4 teaspoon grated nutmeg
- Salt and pepper, to taste
- 1/4 cup grated Parmesan cheese (optional, for added flavor)

Instructions:

Prepare the Spinach:
- Rinse the spinach leaves thoroughly under cold water to remove any dirt or grit.
- Trim off any tough stems or thick veins from the spinach leaves.

Cook the Spinach:
- In a large skillet or pot, melt 1 tablespoon of butter over medium heat.
- Add the minced garlic and sauté for 1 minute until fragrant.
- Add the fresh spinach leaves to the skillet, a handful at a time, and cook until wilted. Continue adding more spinach until all the leaves are wilted. This should only take a few minutes.
- Once the spinach is wilted, transfer it to a colander or sieve to drain excess liquid. Press down gently with a spoon to remove as much liquid as possible.

Make the Cream Sauce:
- In the same skillet, melt the remaining 1 tablespoon of butter over medium heat.
- Sprinkle the flour over the melted butter and whisk continuously to form a smooth paste (roux).
- Gradually pour in the milk or heavy cream, whisking constantly to prevent lumps from forming.
- Cook the mixture for 2-3 minutes until it thickens and becomes smooth and creamy.

Combine Spinach and Cream Sauce:
- Add the drained spinach back to the skillet with the creamy sauce.
- Stir well to coat the spinach with the sauce.

- Season with grated nutmeg, salt, and pepper to taste.
- If using, sprinkle grated Parmesan cheese over the creamed spinach and stir to incorporate.

Serve:
- Transfer the creamed spinach to a serving dish.
- Serve hot as a delicious side dish.

Tips:

- For a lighter version, you can use low-fat milk or half-and-half instead of heavy cream.
- Adjust the consistency of the cream sauce by adding more milk or cream if needed.
- Feel free to customize the dish by adding a pinch of cayenne pepper or a squeeze of lemon juice for extra flavor.
- Leftover creamed spinach can be stored in an airtight container in the refrigerator for up to 3 days. Reheat gently on the stovetop or in the microwave before serving.

Creamed spinach is a classic and comforting side dish that's perfect for holiday dinners or weeknight meals. Enjoy the creamy texture and delicious flavor of this simple yet satisfying dish!

Apple Walnut Salad with Maple Vinaigrette

Ingredients:

For the Salad:

- 6 cups mixed salad greens (such as spinach, arugula, or mixed baby lettuces)
- 2 apples, cored and thinly sliced (use your favorite variety)
- 1/2 cup chopped walnuts, toasted
- 1/4 cup dried cranberries or raisins
- 1/4 cup crumbled feta cheese (optional, for added flavor)
- Salt and pepper, to taste

For the Maple Vinaigrette:

- 1/4 cup olive oil
- 2 tablespoons apple cider vinegar
- 1 tablespoon pure maple syrup
- 1 teaspoon Dijon mustard
- Salt and pepper, to taste

Instructions:

Prepare the Salad Ingredients:
- In a large salad bowl, combine the mixed salad greens, sliced apples, toasted walnuts, dried cranberries or raisins, and crumbled feta cheese (if using).
- Season with a pinch of salt and pepper, to taste.

Make the Maple Vinaigrette:
- In a small bowl or jar, whisk together the olive oil, apple cider vinegar, pure maple syrup, Dijon mustard, salt, and pepper until well combined.
- Alternatively, you can shake the ingredients together in a tightly sealed jar to emulsify the dressing.

Assemble the Salad:
- Drizzle the maple vinaigrette over the salad ingredients in the bowl.
- Toss the salad gently with clean hands or salad tongs until everything is evenly coated with the dressing.

Serve:
- Divide the apple walnut salad onto serving plates or bowls.

- If desired, garnish with additional toasted walnuts, dried cranberries, or crumbled feta cheese on top.
- Serve immediately as a refreshing and flavorful salad.

Tips:

- To toast the walnuts, spread them in a single layer on a baking sheet and toast in a preheated oven at 350°F (175°C) for 5-7 minutes, or until fragrant and lightly golden. Watch them closely to prevent burning.
- Feel free to customize the salad by using different types of apples (such as Honeycrisp, Gala, or Granny Smith) and adjusting the amount of walnuts, dried fruit, or cheese according to your taste preferences.
- Leftover salad can be stored in an airtight container in the refrigerator (without dressing) for 1-2 days. Add dressing just before serving to keep the salad fresh and crisp.

Enjoy this delicious apple walnut salad with maple vinaigrette as a vibrant and satisfying addition to your meal. It's perfect for gatherings, potlucks, or as a healthy lunch option!

Caesar Salad with Homemade Dressing

Ingredients:

For the Caesar Dressing:

- 2-3 anchovy fillets, minced (or 1-2 teaspoons anchovy paste)
- 2 cloves garlic, minced
- 1 teaspoon Dijon mustard
- 2 tablespoons fresh lemon juice
- 1/2 cup mayonnaise
- 1/4 cup grated Parmesan cheese
- 2 tablespoons extra-virgin olive oil
- Salt and black pepper, to taste

For the Salad:

- 1 large head of romaine lettuce, washed and chopped
- 1 cup croutons (homemade or store-bought)
- 1/4 cup grated Parmesan cheese (plus extra for garnish)
- Optional: Grilled chicken, shrimp, or salmon for a protein boost

Instructions:

Prepare the Caesar Dressing:
- In a small bowl, whisk together the minced anchovy fillets (or anchovy paste), minced garlic, Dijon mustard, and fresh lemon juice until well combined.
- Add the mayonnaise and grated Parmesan cheese to the bowl, and whisk until smooth and creamy.
- Gradually drizzle in the extra-virgin olive oil while whisking continuously to emulsify the dressing.
- Season with salt and black pepper, to taste. Adjust the acidity with more lemon juice if desired.

Assemble the Salad:
- In a large salad bowl, combine the chopped romaine lettuce with the croutons and grated Parmesan cheese.
- If adding protein (such as grilled chicken, shrimp, or salmon), place it on top of the salad.

Dress the Salad:
- Drizzle the homemade Caesar dressing over the salad ingredients.

- Toss the salad gently with clean hands or salad tongs until everything is evenly coated with the dressing.

Serve:
- Divide the Caesar salad onto individual plates or bowls.
- Garnish with extra grated Parmesan cheese on top.
- Serve immediately as a delicious and satisfying salad.

Tips:

- If you prefer a smoother dressing, you can blend all the dressing ingredients in a blender or food processor until creamy.
- For vegetarian Caesar salad, you can omit the anchovies or use a vegan alternative.
- Customize the salad by adding additional toppings such as cherry tomatoes, sliced cucumbers, or avocado slices.

Homemade Caesar salad with fresh dressing is a crowd-pleasing dish that's perfect for lunch, dinner, or as a side at gatherings. Enjoy the crisp romaine lettuce, crunchy croutons, and flavorful dressing in this classic Caesar salad!

Deviled Eggs with Bacon

Ingredients:

- 6 large eggs
- 4 slices bacon, cooked until crispy and crumbled
- 3 tablespoons mayonnaise
- 1 tablespoon Dijon mustard
- 1 tablespoon chopped fresh chives (plus extra for garnish)
- Salt and pepper, to taste
- Paprika, for garnish

Instructions:

Hard-Boil the Eggs:
- Place the eggs in a saucepan and cover them with cold water.
- Bring the water to a boil over high heat.
- Once boiling, cover the saucepan with a lid and remove it from the heat.
- Let the eggs sit in the hot water for 10-12 minutes.
- Drain the hot water and immediately transfer the eggs to a bowl of ice water to cool completely.
- Once cooled, peel the eggs and slice them in half lengthwise.

Prepare the Egg Yolk Filling:
- Carefully remove the egg yolks from the halved eggs and place them in a separate bowl.
- Mash the egg yolks with a fork until they are smooth.

Make the Deviled Egg Filling:
- To the mashed egg yolks, add the mayonnaise, Dijon mustard, chopped fresh chives, and crumbled bacon.
- Season with salt and pepper, to taste.
- Mix everything together until well combined and creamy. Adjust the ingredients to achieve your desired taste and texture.

Fill the Egg Whites:
- Spoon or pipe the deviled egg filling back into the hollowed egg whites.
- You can use a piping bag fitted with a star tip for an elegant presentation, or simply spoon the filling into the egg whites.

Garnish and Serve:
- Sprinkle paprika over the filled deviled eggs for a pop of color and flavor.
- Garnish with additional chopped chives and crumbled bacon on top.
- Arrange the deviled eggs on a serving platter and serve chilled.

Tips:

- For perfectly cooked hard-boiled eggs that are easy to peel, use eggs that are not super fresh (about a week old) and follow the boiling and cooling method described.
- You can make the deviled egg filling ahead of time and keep it covered in the refrigerator. Fill the egg whites just before serving for the freshest presentation.
- Experiment with different variations by adding ingredients like minced pickles, hot sauce, or shredded cheese to the deviled egg filling.

Deviled eggs with bacon are sure to be a hit at any gathering or party. Enjoy these flavorful and creamy appetizers with a delightful bacon twist!

Cheese Platter with Assorted Crackers

Ingredients:

Cheeses:

- A selection of cheeses (choose 3-5 varieties for variety), such as:
  - Brie or Camembert
  - Sharp cheddar
  - Gouda
  - Blue cheese (e.g., Roquefort or Gorgonzola)
  - Goat cheese (chevre)
- Consider adding one soft, one semi-soft, one semi-hard, and one hard cheese for variety.

Accompaniments:

- Assorted crackers (such as water crackers, whole grain crackers, or artisanal crisps)
- Sliced baguette or breadsticks
- Fresh fruit (grapes, sliced apples, pears, or figs)
- Dried fruit (apricots, dates, or cranberries)
- Nuts (almonds, walnuts, or pecans)
- Olives or cornichons (small pickles)
- Honey or fruit preserves (optional, for drizzling over cheese)
- Fresh herbs (rosemary sprigs or thyme) for garnish

Instructions:

Choose and Arrange Cheeses:
- Start by selecting a variety of cheeses with different textures and flavors. Arrange them on a large serving platter or wooden board.
- Place each cheese in a separate section of the platter, leaving space between them for accompaniments.

Prepare Accompaniments:
- Arrange the assorted crackers, sliced baguette, or breadsticks around the cheeses on the platter.
- Place small bowls or ramekins filled with honey, fruit preserves, or olives among the cheeses for easy access.

Add Fresh and Dried Fruit:

- Arrange fresh fruit (grapes, sliced apples, pears, or figs) around the cheeses for color and freshness.
- Scatter dried fruit (apricots, dates, or cranberries) and nuts (almonds, walnuts, or pecans) around the platter for added texture and flavor.

Garnish and Serve:
- Garnish the cheese platter with fresh herbs like rosemary sprigs or thyme for a decorative touch.
- Serve the cheese platter at room temperature, allowing the cheeses to soften and develop full flavor.
- Encourage guests to try different combinations of cheeses, crackers, fruits, and condiments.

Tips:

- Include a variety of flavors and textures to appeal to different tastes.
- Label each cheese on the platter so guests know what they are trying.
- Let the cheeses sit at room temperature for 30 minutes to 1 hour before serving to enhance their flavors.
- Have small cheese knives or spreaders available for guests to serve themselves.

A well-curated cheese platter with assorted crackers is perfect for entertaining guests or enjoying as a special treat. It's a versatile and elegant appetizer that's sure to impress! Adjust the selection based on personal preferences and enjoy exploring different flavor combinations.

Fresh Dinner Rolls

Ingredients:

- 4 cups all-purpose flour
- 2 tablespoons granulated sugar
- 1 teaspoon salt
- 2 1/4 teaspoons (1 packet) active dry yeast
- 1 cup warm water (110°F to 115°F or 43°C to 46°C)
- 1/4 cup unsalted butter, melted
- 1 large egg

Optional Toppings:

- Melted butter, for brushing
- Sea salt or sesame seeds, for sprinkling

Instructions:

Activate the Yeast:
- In a small bowl, dissolve the yeast and sugar in warm water. Let it sit for 5-10 minutes until foamy.

Mix the Dough:
- In a large mixing bowl or the bowl of a stand mixer fitted with a dough hook, combine the flour and salt.
- Add the yeast mixture, melted butter, and egg to the flour mixture.
- Mix on low speed until the dough starts to come together.

Knead the Dough:
- Continue kneading the dough for 5-7 minutes, either by hand on a lightly floured surface or using the dough hook attachment on medium-low speed, until the dough is smooth and elastic. Add more flour if the dough is too sticky.

First Rise:
- Place the dough in a lightly greased bowl, turning once to coat the dough with oil.
- Cover the bowl with a clean kitchen towel or plastic wrap and let the dough rise in a warm, draft-free place for 1-1.5 hours, or until doubled in size.

Shape the Rolls:

- Punch down the dough to release air bubbles. Divide the dough into 12 equal portions and shape each portion into a smooth ball.
- Place the dough balls in a greased 9x13-inch baking pan, spacing them evenly apart.

Second Rise:
- Cover the pan with a clean kitchen towel or plastic wrap and let the dough rise for another 30-45 minutes, or until the rolls are puffy and doubled in size.

Preheat the Oven:
- Meanwhile, preheat your oven to 375°F (190°C).

Bake the Rolls:
- Once the rolls have risen, bake them in the preheated oven for 15-20 minutes, or until golden brown on top and cooked through.
- If desired, brush the warm rolls with melted butter and sprinkle with sea salt or sesame seeds for extra flavor.

Serve:
- Transfer the freshly baked dinner rolls to a wire rack to cool slightly before serving.
- Enjoy the warm and fluffy dinner rolls with butter or alongside your favorite dishes.

Tips:

- For a richer flavor, you can substitute some of the water with milk.
- Customize the rolls by adding herbs (such as rosemary or thyme) or grated cheese to the dough before shaping.
- Store leftover dinner rolls in an airtight container at room temperature for 2-3 days. Reheat in the oven or microwave before serving.

Homemade fresh dinner rolls are a delightful addition to any meal. Serve them warm and enjoy the comforting aroma and soft texture of these delicious rolls!

Cranberry Orange Scones

Ingredients:

- 2 cups all-purpose flour
- 1/4 cup granulated sugar
- 1 tablespoon baking powder
- 1/2 teaspoon salt
- Zest of 1 orange
- 1/2 cup (1 stick) cold unsalted butter, cut into small cubes
- 1/2 cup dried cranberries
- 1/2 cup buttermilk (or substitute with milk)
- 1 large egg
- 1 teaspoon vanilla extract
- 2 tablespoons freshly squeezed orange juice
- Optional: Additional sugar for sprinkling on top

Instructions:

Preheat the Oven:
- Preheat your oven to 400°F (200°C). Line a baking sheet with parchment paper or silicone baking mat.

Prepare the Dry Ingredients:
- In a large bowl, whisk together the flour, sugar, baking powder, salt, and orange zest.

Cut in the Butter:
- Add the cold cubed butter to the flour mixture.
- Use a pastry cutter, fork, or your fingertips to cut the butter into the flour until the mixture resembles coarse crumbs. Some larger pea-sized pieces of butter are okay.

Add Cranberries:
- Stir in the dried cranberries until evenly distributed in the flour mixture.

Combine Wet Ingredients:
- In a separate bowl, whisk together the buttermilk, egg, vanilla extract, and orange juice.

Mix the Dough:
- Pour the wet ingredients into the flour mixture.
- Stir with a fork or wooden spoon until the dough starts to come together. It will be slightly shaggy.

Shape the Scones:

- Transfer the dough onto a lightly floured surface.
- Gently knead the dough a few times until it comes together. Do not overwork the dough.
- Pat the dough into a circle about 8 inches (20 cm) in diameter and 1 inch (2.5 cm) thick.

Cut the Dough:
- Use a sharp knife or a bench scraper to cut the dough into 8 equal wedges.

Bake the Scones:
- Place the scones on the prepared baking sheet, spaced a few inches apart.
- Optional: Brush the tops of the scones with a little buttermilk or milk and sprinkle with sugar for a golden crust.
- Bake in the preheated oven for 15-18 minutes, or until the scones are golden brown on top and cooked through.

Cool and Serve:
- Transfer the baked scones to a wire rack to cool slightly.
- Serve warm or at room temperature. Enjoy your cranberry orange scones with a cup of tea or coffee!

Tips:

- For extra citrus flavor, you can add a tablespoon of orange zest to the wet ingredients along with the juice.
- If you don't have buttermilk, you can make a quick substitute by adding 1/2 tablespoon of vinegar or lemon juice to 1/2 cup of milk and letting it sit for 5 minutes.
- Store leftover scones in an airtight container at room temperature for up to 2-3 days. They can also be frozen for longer storage.

These cranberry orange scones are tender, buttery, and bursting with flavor. They make a wonderful homemade treat that's sure to impress your family and friends. Enjoy baking and savoring these delightful scones!

Pumpkin Pie with Whipped Cream

Ingredients:

For the Pumpkin Pie:

- 1 homemade or store-bought pie crust (9-inch)
- 1 can (15 ounces) pumpkin puree
- 3/4 cup granulated sugar
- 1 teaspoon ground cinnamon
- 1/2 teaspoon ground ginger
- 1/4 teaspoon ground cloves
- 1/2 teaspoon salt
- 2 large eggs
- 1 can (12 ounces) evaporated milk

For the Whipped Cream:

- 1 cup heavy cream, chilled
- 2 tablespoons powdered sugar
- 1/2 teaspoon vanilla extract

Instructions:

For the Pumpkin Pie:

Preheat the Oven:
- Preheat your oven to 425°F (220°C).

Prepare the Pie Crust:
- Roll out the pie crust and fit it into a 9-inch pie dish. Trim and crimp the edges as desired.

Make the Pumpkin Filling:
- In a large mixing bowl, whisk together the pumpkin puree, granulated sugar, cinnamon, ginger, cloves, and salt.
- Add the eggs and beat well until combined.
- Gradually stir in the evaporated milk until the mixture is smooth and well blended.

Fill the Pie Crust:
- Pour the pumpkin filling into the prepared pie crust.

Bake the Pie:
- Place the pie in the preheated oven and bake for 15 minutes.

- Reduce the oven temperature to 350°F (175°C) and continue baking for 40-50 minutes, or until the filling is set and a knife inserted near the center comes out clean.
- If the crust edges start to brown too quickly, you can cover them with foil or a pie crust shield halfway through baking.

Cool and Serve:
- Allow the pumpkin pie to cool completely on a wire rack before serving.
- Serve slices of pumpkin pie with freshly whipped cream on top.

For the Whipped Cream:

Chill the Mixing Bowl and Whisk:
- Place a mixing bowl and whisk attachment (or a hand whisk) in the refrigerator for 10-15 minutes to chill.

Whip the Cream:
- Pour the chilled heavy cream into the chilled mixing bowl.
- Begin whipping the cream on medium-high speed until it starts to thicken.

Add Sweetener and Flavoring:
- Gradually add the powdered sugar and vanilla extract to the whipped cream.
- Continue whipping until stiff peaks form. Be careful not to over-whip.

Serve:
- Dollop or pipe the freshly whipped cream onto slices of pumpkin pie just before serving.
- Enjoy your pumpkin pie with delicious homemade whipped cream!

Tips:

- For a decorative touch, sprinkle a little ground cinnamon or nutmeg over the whipped cream.
- Store leftover pumpkin pie in the refrigerator. It can be enjoyed cold or at room temperature.
- Make the whipped cream just before serving for the best texture and consistency.

This pumpkin pie with whipped cream is a wonderful dessert for Thanksgiving, holiday gatherings, or any occasion where you want to savor the flavors of fall. Enjoy the creamy pumpkin filling and light, airy whipped cream with each delightful bite!

Pecan Pie

Ingredients:

For the Pie Crust:

- 1 homemade or store-bought pie crust (9-inch), unbaked

For the Pecan Filling:

- 1 cup granulated sugar
- 1 cup light corn syrup
- 3 large eggs
- 1/4 cup unsalted butter, melted
- 1 teaspoon vanilla extract
- 1/4 teaspoon salt
- 1 1/2 cups pecan halves

Instructions:

Preheat the Oven:
- Preheat your oven to 350°F (175°C).

Prepare the Pie Crust:
- Roll out the pie crust and fit it into a 9-inch pie dish. Trim and crimp the edges as desired.

Make the Pecan Filling:
- In a large mixing bowl, whisk together the granulated sugar, corn syrup, eggs, melted butter, vanilla extract, and salt until well combined.

Add Pecans:
- Stir in the pecan halves until evenly coated with the filling mixture.

Fill the Pie Crust:
- Pour the pecan filling into the prepared pie crust, spreading the pecans evenly across the crust.

Bake the Pie:
- Place the pie in the preheated oven and bake for 50-60 minutes, or until the filling is set and the top is golden brown.
- If the edges of the pie crust start to brown too quickly, you can cover them with foil halfway through baking.

Cool and Serve:
- Allow the pecan pie to cool completely on a wire rack before serving.

- Serve slices of pecan pie on their own or with a dollop of whipped cream or a scoop of vanilla ice cream.

Tips:

- If you prefer a deeper flavor, you can substitute dark corn syrup for the light corn syrup.
- Toasting the pecans before adding them to the filling can enhance their flavor. Simply spread the pecans on a baking sheet and toast in the oven at 350°F (175°C) for about 5-7 minutes, or until fragrant.
- Allow the pecan pie to cool completely before slicing to ensure the filling sets properly.
- Store leftover pecan pie in the refrigerator. It can be enjoyed cold or at room temperature.

This homemade pecan pie is a decadent and delicious dessert that's perfect for special occasions or holiday gatherings. Enjoy the sweet, nutty flavors and rich texture of this Southern classic!

Classic Apple Pie

Ingredients:

For the Pie Crust:

- 2 1/2 cups all-purpose flour
- 1 teaspoon salt
- 1 tablespoon granulated sugar
- 1 cup unsalted butter, cold and cut into small pieces
- 6-8 tablespoons ice water

For the Apple Filling:

- 6-7 large apples (such as Granny Smith, Honeycrisp, or Fuji), peeled, cored, and sliced
- 1/2 cup granulated sugar
- 1/4 cup packed light brown sugar
- 2 tablespoons all-purpose flour
- 1 teaspoon ground cinnamon
- 1/4 teaspoon ground nutmeg
- 1/4 teaspoon salt
- 1 tablespoon fresh lemon juice
- 2 tablespoons unsalted butter, cut into small pieces

For Assembly:

- 1 egg, beaten (for egg wash)
- 1 tablespoon granulated sugar (for sprinkling)

Instructions:

For the Pie Crust:

Prepare the Dough:
- In a large bowl, whisk together the flour, salt, and sugar.
- Add the cold butter pieces to the flour mixture and use a pastry cutter or fork to cut the butter into the flour until the mixture resembles coarse crumbs.
- Gradually add the ice water, one tablespoon at a time, mixing gently with a fork or your hands until the dough comes together and forms a rough ball.

- Divide the dough in half, shape each half into a flat disk, wrap in plastic wrap, and refrigerate for at least 1 hour (or up to overnight).

For the Apple Filling:

Prepare the Apples:
- In a large bowl, toss the sliced apples with lemon juice to prevent browning.

Mix the Filling:
- In a separate bowl, combine the granulated sugar, brown sugar, flour, cinnamon, nutmeg, and salt.
- Add the sugar mixture to the sliced apples and toss until the apples are evenly coated.

For Assembly:

Preheat the Oven:
- Preheat your oven to 375°F (190°C). Place a baking sheet in the oven to preheat as well.

Roll Out the Pie Crust:
- On a lightly floured surface, roll out one disk of dough into a 12-inch circle. Transfer the rolled dough to a 9-inch pie dish, gently pressing it into the bottom and up the sides.

Fill the Pie:
- Pour the apple filling into the prepared pie crust, mounding the apples slightly in the center. Dot the top of the filling with small pieces of butter.

Roll Out the Top Crust:
- Roll out the second disk of dough into a 12-inch circle. Carefully place it over the apples.

Seal and Crimp:
- Trim the excess dough, leaving about a 1-inch overhang. Fold the overhang under the bottom crust, then crimp the edges using your fingers or a fork to seal the pie.

Ventilation:
- Cut a few slits in the top crust to allow steam to escape during baking.

Bake the Pie:
- Brush the top crust with beaten egg and sprinkle with granulated sugar.
- Place the pie on the preheated baking sheet in the oven.
- Bake for 45-55 minutes, or until the crust is golden brown and the filling is bubbly.

Cool and Serve:
- Allow the apple pie to cool on a wire rack for at least 2 hours before slicing.
- Serve slices of apple pie warm or at room temperature, optionally with a scoop of vanilla ice cream.

Tips:

- Use a combination of tart and sweet apples for the best flavor and texture in the filling.
- Make sure the butter in the pie crust is cold to achieve a flaky texture.
- If the edges of the pie crust start to brown too quickly during baking, cover them with foil halfway through baking.
- Store leftover apple pie covered in the refrigerator. Reheat before serving if desired.

Enjoy this classic homemade apple pie with its buttery crust and spiced apple filling. It's perfect for holidays, gatherings, or anytime you're craving a comforting dessert!

Chocolate Yule Log Cake

Ingredients:

For the Sponge Cake:

- 4 large eggs, at room temperature
- 3/4 cup granulated sugar
- 1 teaspoon vanilla extract
- 1/2 cup all-purpose flour
- 1/4 cup unsweetened cocoa powder
- 1/2 teaspoon baking powder
- 1/4 teaspoon salt
- Powdered sugar (for dusting)

For the Chocolate Filling:

- 1 1/2 cups heavy cream
- 10 ounces (about 1 2/3 cups) semi-sweet or dark chocolate chips
- 2 tablespoons unsalted butter

For Decoration:

- Powdered sugar, for dusting
- Cocoa powder, for dusting
- Fresh berries, mint leaves, or edible decorations (optional)

Instructions:

For the Sponge Cake:

Preheat the Oven:
- Preheat your oven to 350°F (175°C). Line a 10x15-inch jelly roll pan with parchment paper, leaving an overhang on the sides.

Make the Sponge Cake:
- In a large mixing bowl, beat the eggs and granulated sugar with an electric mixer on high speed until pale, fluffy, and tripled in volume (about 5-7 minutes).
- Beat in the vanilla extract.

Sift Dry Ingredients:
- In a separate bowl, sift together the flour, cocoa powder, baking powder, and salt.

Fold Dry Ingredients:

- Gradually sift the dry ingredients over the beaten egg mixture, gently folding with a spatula until just combined. Be careful not to deflate the batter.

Bake the Cake:
- Pour the batter into the prepared jelly roll pan and spread it evenly.
- Bake for 12-15 minutes or until the cake springs back when lightly touched.

Roll the Cake:
- While the cake is still warm, dust the top with powdered sugar.
- Carefully invert the cake onto a clean kitchen towel dusted with powdered sugar.
- Gently peel off the parchment paper.
- Starting from one short end, roll the cake and towel together into a tight log. Place seam side down and let it cool completely.

For the Chocolate Filling:

Prepare the Chocolate Ganache:
- In a medium saucepan, heat the heavy cream over medium heat until it just starts to simmer (do not boil).
- Remove from heat and add the chocolate chips and butter. Let it sit for a few minutes, then stir until smooth and glossy.

Cool the Ganache:
- Let the chocolate ganache cool to room temperature, stirring occasionally. It should thicken to a spreadable consistency.

Assemble the Yule Log Cake:

Unroll the Cake:
- Carefully unroll the cooled cake from the towel.

Spread the Filling:
- Spread the cooled chocolate ganache evenly over the cake, leaving a small border around the edges.

Roll the Cake:
- Starting from the same short end, roll the cake tightly without the towel. Place seam side down on a serving platter.

Decorate:
- Use a fork to create a bark-like texture on the surface of the cake.
- Dust the Yule log with powdered sugar and cocoa powder to resemble snow and bark.
- Decorate with fresh berries, mint leaves, or other edible decorations if desired.

Chill and Serve:
- Refrigerate the Chocolate Yule Log Cake for at least 1-2 hours before serving to set the filling.
- Slice and serve chilled.

Tips:

- Make sure to roll the cake while it's still warm to prevent cracking.
- Use a good quality chocolate for the filling to achieve a rich and smooth ganache.
- Customize the decorations based on your preference and creativity.

Enjoy this Chocolate Yule Log Cake as a stunning centerpiece dessert for your holiday celebrations! It's sure to impress with its delicious chocolate flavor and festive appearance.

Gingerbread Cookies

Ingredients:

- 3 cups all-purpose flour
- 1 teaspoon baking soda
- 1/4 teaspoon salt
- 1 tablespoon ground ginger
- 1 1/2 teaspoons ground cinnamon
- 1/2 teaspoon ground cloves
- 1/2 teaspoon ground nutmeg
- 3/4 cup unsalted butter, softened
- 1/2 cup granulated sugar
- 1/2 cup packed brown sugar
- 1 large egg
- 1/2 cup molasses
- 1 teaspoon vanilla extract

For Decorating (Optional):

- Royal icing or icing sugar mixed with water
- Assorted sprinkles, candies, or edible decorations

Instructions:

Preheat the Oven:
- Preheat your oven to 350°F (175°C) and line baking sheets with parchment paper.

Mix Dry Ingredients:
- In a medium bowl, whisk together the flour, baking soda, salt, ginger, cinnamon, cloves, and nutmeg. Set aside.

Cream Butter and Sugars:
- In a large mixing bowl, beat the softened butter, granulated sugar, and brown sugar together until light and fluffy.

Add Wet Ingredients:
- Beat in the egg, molasses, and vanilla extract until well combined.

Combine Wet and Dry Ingredients:
- Gradually add the dry ingredient mixture to the wet ingredients, mixing until a dough forms. You may need to use your hands to fully incorporate the flour mixture into the dough.

Chill the Dough:
- Divide the dough into two equal portions, flatten each into a disk, and wrap in plastic wrap.
- Refrigerate the dough for at least 1 hour (or up to overnight) to firm it up.

Roll Out the Dough:
- On a lightly floured surface, roll out one portion of the chilled dough to about 1/4-inch thickness.
- Use cookie cutters to cut out shapes (such as gingerbread men, stars, or hearts) and transfer them to the prepared baking sheets, leaving space between each cookie.

Bake the Cookies:
- Bake the cookies in the preheated oven for 8-10 minutes, or until the edges are set.
- Let the cookies cool on the baking sheets for a few minutes before transferring them to wire racks to cool completely.

Decorate (Optional):
- Once the cookies are completely cooled, decorate them using royal icing or a simple icing made from icing sugar mixed with water.
- Add assorted sprinkles, candies, or edible decorations to embellish the cookies.

Enjoy:
- Allow the icing to set before serving and enjoying these delicious gingerbread cookies!

Tips:

- For softer cookies, roll out the dough slightly thicker.
- If the dough becomes too soft or sticky while working with it, return it to the refrigerator to chill for a few minutes.
- Store decorated gingerbread cookies in an airtight container at room temperature. They can be enjoyed for several days.

These homemade gingerbread cookies are a festive and flavorful treat that everyone will love. Have fun decorating them and spreading holiday cheer with these delicious cookies!

Peppermint Bark

Ingredients:

- 12 ounces (about 2 cups) semisweet or dark chocolate, chopped
- 12 ounces (about 2 cups) white chocolate, chopped
- 1 teaspoon vegetable oil or coconut oil, divided
- 1/2 teaspoon peppermint extract, divided
- 4-6 candy canes or peppermint candies, crushed

Instructions:

Prepare Baking Sheet:
- Line a baking sheet with parchment paper or wax paper.

Melt Semisweet/Dark Chocolate:
- In a microwave-safe bowl, microwave the chopped semisweet or dark chocolate with 1/2 teaspoon of vegetable oil (or coconut oil) in 30-second intervals, stirring after each interval, until the chocolate is melted and smooth.
- Stir in 1/4 teaspoon of peppermint extract.

Spread Chocolate on Baking Sheet:
- Pour the melted semisweet/dark chocolate onto the prepared baking sheet.
- Use a spatula to spread the chocolate evenly into a thin layer, about 1/4-inch thick. Tap the baking sheet gently on the counter to smooth the surface.

Chill Semisweet/Dark Chocolate:
- Place the baking sheet in the refrigerator for about 20-30 minutes, or until the chocolate is set.

Melt White Chocolate:
- In another microwave-safe bowl, microwave the chopped white chocolate with 1/2 teaspoon of vegetable oil (or coconut oil) in 30-second intervals, stirring after each interval, until the chocolate is melted and smooth.
- Stir in 1/4 teaspoon of peppermint extract.

Spread White Chocolate on Semisweet/Dark Chocolate Layer:
- Pour the melted white chocolate over the chilled semisweet/dark chocolate layer.
- Use a spatula to spread the white chocolate evenly over the semisweet/dark chocolate layer.

Sprinkle Crushed Peppermint:

- Immediately sprinkle the crushed candy canes or peppermint candies evenly over the white chocolate layer, pressing them gently into the chocolate.

Chill and Set:
- Return the baking sheet to the refrigerator for another 20-30 minutes, or until the peppermint bark is completely set and firm.

Break Into Pieces:
- Once set, remove the peppermint bark from the refrigerator.
- Use your hands or a knife to break the bark into pieces of various sizes and shapes.

Serve or Gift:
- Serve the peppermint bark on a festive platter or package it in gift bags or boxes for gifting.

Tips:

- Use high-quality chocolate for the best flavor and texture.
- Adjust the amount of peppermint extract and crushed peppermint to suit your taste preferences.
- Store peppermint bark in an airtight container in the refrigerator for up to 2 weeks.

Enjoy this homemade peppermint bark as a delightful holiday treat or give it as a thoughtful homemade gift to friends and family. It's festive, easy to make, and always a hit during the holiday season!

Eggnog Cheesecake

Ingredients:

For the Crust:

- 1 1/2 cups graham cracker crumbs
- 1/4 cup granulated sugar
- 1/2 cup unsalted butter, melted

For the Cheesecake Filling:

- 24 ounces (3 packages) cream cheese, softened
- 1 cup granulated sugar
- 3 large eggs
- 1 cup eggnog
- 1/4 cup all-purpose flour
- 1 teaspoon vanilla extract
- 1/2 teaspoon ground nutmeg
- Optional: 1/4 cup dark rum (for a boozy version)

For Topping (Optional):

- Whipped cream
- Ground nutmeg
- Cinnamon sticks or cinnamon powder (for garnish)

Instructions:

For the Crust:

   Preheat the Oven:
   - Preheat your oven to 325°F (160°C). Wrap the outside of a 9-inch springform pan with aluminum foil to prevent water from leaking into the pan during baking.

   Prepare the Crust:
   - In a medium bowl, combine the graham cracker crumbs, sugar, and melted butter. Mix until the crumbs are evenly coated with butter.

   Press into Pan:
   - Press the crumb mixture firmly into the bottom of the prepared springform pan to form an even crust.

For the Cheesecake Filling:

Beat Cream Cheese and Sugar:
- In a large mixing bowl, beat the softened cream cheese and sugar together until smooth and creamy.

Add Eggs:
- Add the eggs one at a time, beating well after each addition.

Add Eggnog and Flour:
- Stir in the eggnog, flour, vanilla extract, and ground nutmeg until well combined.
- Optional: Stir in the dark rum for a boozy eggnog flavor.

Pour Over Crust:
- Pour the cheesecake batter over the prepared crust in the springform pan.

Baking the Cheesecake:

Prepare Water Bath:
- Place the springform pan inside a larger baking pan or roasting pan. Fill the larger pan with hot water until it reaches halfway up the sides of the springform pan.

Bake:
- Carefully transfer the pans to the preheated oven.
- Bake the cheesecake for 60-70 minutes, or until the edges are set and the center is slightly jiggly.

Cool and Chill:
- Turn off the oven and leave the cheesecake in the oven with the door slightly ajar for 1 hour.
- Remove the cheesecake from the water bath and let it cool completely on a wire rack.
- Refrigerate the cheesecake for at least 4 hours or overnight to chill and set.

Serving the Cheesecake:

Remove from Pan:
- Carefully remove the sides of the springform pan.

Decorate:
- Before serving, garnish the eggnog cheesecake with whipped cream, a sprinkle of ground nutmeg, and cinnamon sticks or a dusting of cinnamon powder, if desired.

Slice and Serve:
- Slice the cheesecake into wedges and serve chilled.

Tips:

- For best results, use room temperature cream cheese to ensure a smooth and creamy filling.

- To prevent cracks in the cheesecake, avoid overmixing the batter and avoid opening the oven door too frequently during baking.
- Store leftover eggnog cheesecake in the refrigerator for up to 3-4 days.

Enjoy this creamy and festive eggnog cheesecake as a delightful dessert for your holiday gatherings. It's sure to be a hit with eggnog lovers and cheesecake enthusiasts alike!

Linzer Cookies

Ingredients:

For the Cookie Dough:

- 1 cup unsalted butter, softened
- 3/4 cup granulated sugar
- 1 large egg
- 1 teaspoon vanilla extract
- 2 cups all-purpose flour
- 1 cup almond flour (or finely ground almonds)
- 1/2 teaspoon ground cinnamon
- 1/4 teaspoon salt
- Powdered sugar, for dusting

For Filling and Assembly:

- About 1/2 cup raspberry jam (or your favorite jam)
- Additional powdered sugar, for dusting

Instructions:

Making the Cookie Dough:

    Cream Butter and Sugar:
- In a large mixing bowl, beat the softened butter and granulated sugar together until light and fluffy.

    Add Egg and Vanilla:
- Beat in the egg and vanilla extract until well combined.

    Combine Dry Ingredients:
- In a separate bowl, whisk together the all-purpose flour, almond flour (or ground almonds), cinnamon, and salt.

    Mix Dough:
- Gradually add the dry ingredient mixture to the butter mixture, mixing until a dough forms. The dough should come together and be slightly sticky.

    Chill Dough:
- Divide the dough into two equal portions, shape each portion into a disk, wrap in plastic wrap, and refrigerate for at least 1 hour (or up to overnight) until firm.

Baking the Cookies:

Preheat the Oven:
- Preheat your oven to 350°F (175°C). Line baking sheets with parchment paper.

Roll Out Dough:
- On a lightly floured surface, roll out one disk of chilled dough to about 1/4-inch thickness.

Cut Out Shapes:
- Use a round cookie cutter to cut out cookies. For half of the cookies, use a smaller cookie cutter (such as a heart or star shape) to cut out the centers.

Bake:
- Place the cookies on the prepared baking sheets.
- Bake for 10-12 minutes, or until the edges are lightly golden.
- Remove from the oven and let the cookies cool on the baking sheets for a few minutes before transferring them to wire racks to cool completely.

Assembling the Linzer Cookies:

Dust with Powdered Sugar:
- Dust the cookies with the cut-out centers (tops) with powdered sugar.

Spread Jam:
- Spread a thin layer of raspberry jam (or your preferred jam) on the bottom side of each whole cookie (cookies without cut-out centers).

Assemble:
- Place a jam-coated whole cookie on top of each powdered sugar-dusted cookie (with the cut-out center), pressing gently to create sandwich cookies.

Dust Again:
- Dust the assembled Linzer cookies with additional powdered sugar for a finished look.

Serve:
- Arrange the Linzer cookies on a platter and serve.

Tips:
- Make sure the dough is well chilled before rolling and cutting to prevent sticking.
- You can customize the filling by using different flavors of jam, such as apricot, strawberry, or blackberry.

- Store Linzer cookies in an airtight container at room temperature. They can be stored for several days, and the flavors will meld together nicely.

Enjoy these beautiful and delicious Linzer cookies with their delicate almond flavor and sweet jam filling. They're a wonderful addition to any holiday dessert spread or cookie exchange!

Bûche de Noël

Ingredients:

For the Cake:

- 4 large eggs, separated
- 3/4 cup granulated sugar
- 1 teaspoon vanilla extract
- 1/4 cup cocoa powder
- 1/4 cup all-purpose flour
- 1/4 teaspoon salt

For the Filling:

- 1 1/2 cups heavy cream
- 1/4 cup powdered sugar
- 1 teaspoon vanilla extract

For the Chocolate Ganache Frosting:

- 6 ounces semi-sweet chocolate, chopped
- 3/4 cup heavy cream
- 2 tablespoons unsalted butter, softened

For Decoration (Optional):

- Meringue mushrooms (or other decorations)
- Powdered sugar (for dusting)
- Additional chocolate shavings or decorations

Instructions:

Making the Cake:

Preheat the Oven:
- Preheat your oven to 350°F (175°C). Grease a 10x15-inch jelly roll pan and line it with parchment paper.

Prepare the Batter:
- In a large mixing bowl, beat the egg yolks with granulated sugar and vanilla extract until pale and thick.

Add Dry Ingredients:

- Sift in the cocoa powder, flour, and salt into the egg yolk mixture. Gently fold until just combined.

Whip Egg Whites:
- In a separate bowl, beat the egg whites until stiff peaks form.

Fold Egg Whites into Batter:
- Gradually fold the whipped egg whites into the chocolate batter until no streaks remain.

Bake the Cake:
- Spread the batter evenly into the prepared jelly roll pan.
- Bake for 12-15 minutes or until the cake springs back when lightly touched.

Roll the Cake:
- While the cake is still warm, invert it onto a clean kitchen towel dusted with powdered sugar.
- Carefully peel off the parchment paper.
- Roll the cake from the short end along with the towel. Let it cool completely while rolled up.

Making the Filling:

Prepare the Whipped Cream:
- In a mixing bowl, whip the heavy cream with powdered sugar and vanilla extract until stiff peaks form.

Assembling the Bûche de Noël:

Unroll the Cake:
- Carefully unroll the cooled cake from the towel.

Spread the Filling:
- Spread the whipped cream filling evenly over the cake.

Roll the Cake:
- Roll up the cake tightly, starting from one short end.

Make the Chocolate Ganache:
- In a heatproof bowl, combine the chopped chocolate and softened butter.
- In a small saucepan, heat the heavy cream until just simmering.
- Pour the hot cream over the chocolate and let it sit for a few minutes. Stir until smooth and glossy.

Frost the Cake:
- Spread the chocolate ganache over the rolled cake, using a spatula to create a bark-like texture.

Decoration:
- Use a fork to create wood grain patterns on the chocolate ganache.
- Decorate the Bûche de Noël with meringue mushrooms, powdered sugar "snow," and any additional decorations.

Chill and Serve:
- Refrigerate the Bûche de Noël for at least 1-2 hours before serving.
- Slice and serve chilled, enjoying this festive and delicious holiday dessert!

Tips:

- Be gentle when rolling and unrolling the cake to prevent cracking.
- Customize the decorations based on your preference, using edible decorations like meringue mushrooms, fresh berries, or chocolate shavings.
- Store leftovers in the refrigerator. Bûche de Noël can be made a day ahead of time and kept chilled until serving.

Enjoy this beautiful and delicious Bûche de Noël as the centerpiece of your holiday dessert table. It's a delightful treat that will impress your guests and bring festive cheer to your celebrations!

Cranberry Pistachio Biscotti

Ingredients:

- 2 cups all-purpose flour
- 1 teaspoon baking powder
- 1/4 teaspoon salt
- 1/2 cup unsalted butter, softened
- 3/4 cup granulated sugar
- 2 large eggs
- 1 teaspoon vanilla extract
- 1/2 cup dried cranberries
- 1/2 cup shelled pistachios, chopped
- Zest of 1 orange (optional, for added flavor)
- 1 egg white, beaten (for brushing)

Instructions:

Preheat the Oven:
- Preheat your oven to 350°F (175°C). Line a baking sheet with parchment paper.

Mix Dry Ingredients:
- In a medium bowl, whisk together the all-purpose flour, baking powder, and salt. Set aside.

Cream Butter and Sugar:
- In a large mixing bowl, cream together the softened butter and granulated sugar until light and fluffy.

Add Wet Ingredients:
- Beat in the eggs, one at a time, followed by the vanilla extract.

Combine Wet and Dry Ingredients:
- Gradually add the flour mixture to the wet ingredients, mixing until a dough forms.

Fold in Cranberries and Pistachios:
- Gently fold in the dried cranberries, chopped pistachios, and orange zest (if using) into the dough until evenly distributed.

Shape the Dough:
- Divide the dough in half. On a lightly floured surface, shape each half into a log about 12 inches long and 2 inches wide. Place the logs on the prepared baking sheet, spaced apart.

Brush with Egg White:

- Brush the tops and sides of the logs with beaten egg white. This will give the biscotti a nice golden color when baked.

Bake:
- Bake the logs in the preheated oven for 25-30 minutes, or until lightly golden and set.

Cool and Slice:
- Remove the baked logs from the oven and let them cool on the baking sheet for about 10 minutes.
- Reduce the oven temperature to 325°F (160°C).

Slice the Biscotti:
- Transfer the cooled logs to a cutting board. Using a sharp knife, slice each log diagonally into 1/2-inch thick slices.

Second Bake:
- Arrange the biscotti slices cut-side down on the baking sheet.
- Bake for an additional 10-12 minutes, flipping the biscotti halfway through baking, until they are golden and crisp.

Cool and Serve:
- Let the biscotti cool completely on wire racks.
- Once cooled, store the biscotti in an airtight container at room temperature.

Tips:
- Feel free to customize the flavors by using different dried fruits or nuts, such as dried cherries, almonds, or walnuts.
- For extra flavor, you can drizzle melted white or dark chocolate over the cooled biscotti.

Enjoy these homemade cranberry pistachio biscotti with your favorite hot beverage or package them up as a thoughtful homemade gift during the holiday season. They're perfect for sharing and spreading festive cheer!

Spiced Apple Cider

Ingredients:

- 8 cups (64 ounces) apple cider (fresh or store-bought)
- 2 cinnamon sticks
- 4 whole cloves
- 4 whole allspice berries
- 1 orange, sliced (optional)
- 1/4 cup brown sugar or maple syrup (adjust to taste)
- Additional spices (optional): star anise, nutmeg, cardamom pods

Instructions:

Combine Ingredients:
- In a large pot or Dutch oven, combine the apple cider, cinnamon sticks, whole cloves, whole allspice berries, and orange slices.

Add Sweetener:
- Stir in brown sugar or maple syrup to sweeten the cider. Adjust the amount based on your preference for sweetness.

Simmer:
- Place the pot over medium-high heat and bring the cider mixture to a simmer.
- Reduce the heat to low and let the cider simmer gently for 20-30 minutes to allow the flavors to infuse.

Strain:
- Once the cider is infused with spices and flavors, remove the pot from the heat.
- Use a fine-mesh sieve or cheesecloth to strain out the spices and orange slices. Discard the solids.

Serve:
- Ladle the spiced apple cider into mugs or heatproof glasses.
- Optionally, garnish each serving with a cinnamon stick or fresh orange slice for a festive touch.

Enjoy:
- Serve the spiced apple cider warm and enjoy its comforting flavors!

Tips:

- Feel free to adjust the spice quantities based on your taste preferences. You can also experiment with other spices like star anise, nutmeg, or cardamom pods.
- If you prefer a stronger spice flavor, you can let the cider simmer for a longer period of time.
- Leftover spiced apple cider can be stored in the refrigerator for a few days. Reheat gently on the stove or in the microwave before serving.

Spiced apple cider is perfect for holiday gatherings, chilly evenings by the fireplace, or simply as a comforting treat during the fall and winter seasons. It's a wonderful way to enjoy the flavors of the season with family and friends!

Mulled Wine

Ingredients:

- 1 bottle (750 ml) red wine (such as Merlot, Cabernet Sauvignon, or Malbec)
- 1 orange, sliced
- 8 whole cloves
- 2 cinnamon sticks
- 2 star anise
- 1/4 cup honey or brown sugar (adjust to taste)
- 1/2 cup brandy or orange liqueur (optional)
- Additional garnishes (optional): orange peel, cinnamon sticks, star anise

Instructions:

Combine Ingredients:
- In a large pot or saucepan, combine the red wine, sliced orange, whole cloves, cinnamon sticks, and star anise.

Add Sweetener:
- Stir in honey or brown sugar to sweeten the mulled wine. Adjust the amount based on your preference for sweetness.

Heat Gently:
- Place the pot over medium-low heat. Slowly warm the mulled wine mixture, stirring occasionally, until it reaches a gentle simmer. Be careful not to boil the wine.

Simmer:
- Once the wine is simmering, reduce the heat to low and let it simmer gently for 15-20 minutes. This allows the flavors to infuse into the wine.

Add Brandy (Optional):
- If using, stir in brandy or orange liqueur for an extra kick of flavor and warmth. Adjust the amount based on your preference.

Strain and Serve:
- Remove the pot from the heat.
- Use a ladle to strain the mulled wine into heatproof glasses or mugs, discarding the spices and orange slices.

Garnish (Optional):
- Garnish each serving of mulled wine with a twist of orange peel, cinnamon stick, or star anise for a festive touch.

Enjoy:
- Serve the mulled wine warm and enjoy its deliciously spiced flavors!

Tips:

- Use a good-quality red wine for the best flavor. Avoid using overly tannic wines.
- Feel free to adjust the spices and sweeteners based on your taste preferences. You can add more cloves, cinnamon, or honey to suit your liking.
- Keep the heat low while simmering to prevent boiling, which can affect the flavor of the wine.

Mulled wine is a wonderful beverage to serve at holiday parties, cozy gatherings, or simply to enjoy on a chilly evening by the fire. It's guaranteed to warm you up and spread festive cheer!

Festive Holiday Punch

Ingredients:

- 4 cups cranberry juice
- 2 cups orange juice
- 1 cup pineapple juice
- 1/4 cup fresh lemon juice
- 2 cups ginger ale or lemon-lime soda, chilled
- 1 cup sparkling water or club soda, chilled
- Fresh cranberries, orange slices, and mint leaves (for garnish)
- Ice cubes

Instructions:

Combine Fruit Juices:
- In a large punch bowl or pitcher, combine the cranberry juice, orange juice, pineapple juice, and fresh lemon juice. Stir well to mix.

Chill:
- If the fruit juices are not chilled, you can chill the mixture in the refrigerator for 1-2 hours before serving.

Add Sparkling Soda:
- Just before serving, pour in the chilled ginger ale (or lemon-lime soda) and sparkling water (or club soda) into the punch bowl. Stir gently to combine.

Garnish:
- Add ice cubes to the punch bowl to keep the drink cold.
- Garnish the punch with fresh cranberries, orange slices, and mint leaves for a festive presentation.

Serve:
- Ladle the festive holiday punch into glasses filled with ice.
- Make sure each glass gets a good mix of fruit and garnishes.

Enjoy:
- Serve the punch immediately and enjoy its bright and refreshing flavors!

Tips:

- For an extra festive touch, you can freeze cranberries in ice cubes to use as decorative ice cubes in the punch.
- Adjust the sweetness by adding a little honey or simple syrup if desired.

- Feel free to customize the punch by adding sliced apples, pomegranate seeds, or other seasonal fruits.

This festive holiday punch is perfect for entertaining guests and spreading cheer during the holidays. It's a non-alcoholic option that can be enjoyed by all ages. Serve it alongside other holiday treats and appetizers for a memorable gathering!

Sparkling Cranberry Mocktail

Ingredients:

- 1 cup cranberry juice (100% juice, unsweetened)
- 1/2 cup sparkling water or club soda, chilled
- 1 tablespoon fresh lime juice
- 1 tablespoon honey or simple syrup (adjust to taste)
- Ice cubes
- Fresh cranberries and lime slices (for garnish)
- Rosemary sprigs (optional, for garnish)

Instructions:

Prepare Serving Glasses:
- Fill serving glasses with ice cubes to chill.

Mix Mocktail:
- In a mixing glass or pitcher, combine the cranberry juice, sparkling water (or club soda), fresh lime juice, and honey (or simple syrup). Stir well to combine.

Taste and Adjust:
- Taste the mocktail and adjust the sweetness by adding more honey or simple syrup if desired.

Pour into Glasses:
- Pour the mocktail mixture into the prepared serving glasses over the ice cubes.

Garnish:
- Garnish each glass with a few fresh cranberries, a slice of lime, and a sprig of rosemary (if using). This adds a festive and aromatic touch to the mocktail.

Serve and Enjoy:
- Serve the Sparkling Cranberry Mocktail immediately and enjoy its bright and bubbly flavors!

Tips:

- For an extra festive presentation, you can rim the glasses with sugar or coarse sugar before adding the ice and mocktail mixture.
- Feel free to experiment with different flavors by adding a splash of orange juice or a few drops of vanilla extract to the mocktail.

- To make a larger batch for a party, simply multiply the ingredients accordingly and mix in a pitcher before serving.

This Sparkling Cranberry Mocktail is a perfect beverage option for guests of all ages during holiday gatherings. It's easy to make, visually appealing, and bursting with seasonal flavors. Cheers to a delicious and festive mocktail!

Hot Chocolate with Marshmallows

Ingredients:

- 2 cups milk (any type of milk you prefer: whole milk, almond milk, oat milk, etc.)
- 2 tablespoons unsweetened cocoa powder
- 2 tablespoons granulated sugar (adjust to taste)
- 1/2 teaspoon vanilla extract
- Pinch of salt
- Marshmallows (mini marshmallows or regular marshmallows)

Optional Toppings:

- Whipped cream
- Chocolate shavings
- Cinnamon powder

Instructions:

Warm Milk:
- In a small saucepan, heat the milk over medium heat until it's warm and steaming but not boiling.

Whisk in Cocoa Powder and Sugar:
- Whisk in the unsweetened cocoa powder and granulated sugar until they are fully dissolved and the mixture is smooth.

Add Vanilla and Salt:
- Stir in the vanilla extract and a pinch of salt. This enhances the flavor of the hot chocolate.

Heat Through:
- Continue to heat the hot chocolate mixture, stirring occasionally, until it is hot and steamy. Do not let it boil.

Serve:
- Pour the hot chocolate into mugs.

Add Marshmallows:
- Top each mug of hot chocolate with marshmallows. Use as many marshmallows as you like!

Optional Toppings:
- For extra indulgence, add a dollop of whipped cream on top of the marshmallows.

- Sprinkle with chocolate shavings or a dash of cinnamon powder for additional flavor.

Enjoy:
- Serve the hot chocolate immediately while it's still hot and creamy. Stir before sipping to incorporate the marshmallows into the drink.

Tips:

- Use high-quality cocoa powder for the best flavor.
- Adjust the sweetness by adding more or less sugar according to your taste preferences.
- Feel free to customize your hot chocolate with different toppings like caramel sauce, peppermint extract, or a splash of coffee for a mocha twist.

This homemade hot chocolate with marshmallows is a delightful treat that will warm you up from the inside out. It's perfect for enjoying during the holiday season or any time you crave a comforting and delicious drink. Sit back, relax, and savor every sip of this cozy beverage!

Cinnamon Spiced Nuts

Ingredients:

- 3 cups mixed nuts (such as almonds, pecans, walnuts, cashews)
- 1 egg white
- 1 tablespoon water
- 1/2 cup granulated sugar
- 2 teaspoons ground cinnamon
- 1/2 teaspoon salt
- Optional: 1/4 teaspoon ground nutmeg or ground cloves

Instructions:

Preheat Oven:
- Preheat your oven to 300°F (150°C). Line a baking sheet with parchment paper or lightly grease it.

Prepare Egg White Mixture:
- In a large bowl, whisk together the egg white and water until frothy.

Coat Nuts:
- Add the mixed nuts to the egg white mixture and toss until the nuts are well coated.

Mix Cinnamon Sugar:
- In a separate bowl, combine the granulated sugar, ground cinnamon, salt, and optional ground nutmeg or cloves.

Coat Nuts with Sugar Mixture:
- Sprinkle the cinnamon sugar mixture over the coated nuts and toss until the nuts are evenly coated.

Spread on Baking Sheet:
- Spread the coated nuts in a single layer on the prepared baking sheet.

Bake:
- Bake the nuts in the preheated oven for 30-35 minutes, stirring halfway through, until the nuts are golden and fragrant.

Cool:
- Remove the baking sheet from the oven and let the nuts cool completely on the pan. The nuts will continue to crisp up as they cool.

Serve:
- Once cooled, transfer the cinnamon spiced nuts to a serving bowl or airtight container.

Tips:

- Use a variety of nuts for a delicious mix of flavors and textures.
- Make sure to spread the nuts in a single layer on the baking sheet to ensure even baking.
- Customize the spices based on your preference. You can add a hint of nutmeg, cloves, or even cayenne pepper for a spicy kick.
- Store the cinnamon spiced nuts in an airtight container at room temperature for up to 1-2 weeks.

These cinnamon spiced nuts are perfect for snacking, holiday parties, or as a homemade gift. They're crunchy, sweet, and packed with warm cinnamon flavor. Enjoy this festive treat during the holiday season and beyond!

Assorted Holiday Truffles

Ingredients:

For the Truffle Base:

- 12 ounces (340g) good quality semi-sweet or dark chocolate, chopped
- 1 cup heavy cream
- 2 tablespoons unsalted butter, softened
- 1 teaspoon vanilla extract

For Flavor Variations:

- Peppermint Truffles:
    - 1/2 teaspoon peppermint extract
    - Crushed candy canes (for rolling)
- Orange Truffles:
    - Zest of 1 orange
    - Grand Marnier or orange liqueur (optional)
    - Cocoa powder (for rolling)
- Hazelnut Truffles:
    - 1/2 cup finely chopped toasted hazelnuts
    - Nutella or hazelnut spread (optional)
    - Finely chopped hazelnuts (for rolling)
- Coconut Truffles:
    - 1/2 cup shredded coconut, toasted
    - Coconut rum (optional)
    - Toasted coconut flakes (for rolling)

For Coatings:

- Cocoa powder
- Finely chopped nuts (e.g., hazelnuts, almonds)
- Powdered sugar
- Melted chocolate (white or dark)
- Sprinkles or edible glitter

Instructions:

Prepare the Truffle Base:
- Place the chopped chocolate in a heatproof bowl.

- In a small saucepan, heat the heavy cream over medium heat until it just starts to simmer (do not boil).
- Pour the hot cream over the chopped chocolate and let it sit for 1-2 minutes.
- Stir gently until the chocolate is completely melted and smooth.
- Stir in the softened butter and vanilla extract until well combined and creamy.

Divide and Flavor the Truffle Base:
- Divide the chocolate mixture into separate bowls depending on how many flavor variations you want to make.
- Add the flavorings for each variation (e.g., peppermint extract, orange zest, finely chopped hazelnuts, shredded coconut) to the corresponding bowls. Mix well to combine.

Chill the Truffle Mixtures:
- Cover each bowl with plastic wrap and refrigerate until firm, at least 2 hours or overnight.

Shape the Truffles:
- Using a small spoon or melon baller, scoop out small portions of the chilled truffle mixture and roll them into balls using your hands. Place the truffles on a parchment-lined baking sheet.
- If the mixture is too soft to handle, return it to the refrigerator for a short time to firm up.

Coat the Truffles:
- Prepare different coatings in separate bowls or plates (e.g., cocoa powder, chopped nuts, powdered sugar).
- Roll each truffle in the desired coating until evenly coated. Use a fork or dipping tool to remove excess coating.

Decorate (Optional):
- Drizzle melted chocolate over the truffles, or top them with sprinkles or edible glitter for a festive touch.

Chill and Serve:
- Place the coated truffles back on the baking sheet and refrigerate until firm.
- Store the assorted holiday truffles in an airtight container in the refrigerator until ready to serve or gift.

Tips:

- Get creative with flavors and coatings! Experiment with different extracts, liqueurs, and toppings to create a variety of truffles.
- To make the truffles ahead of time, store them in the refrigerator for up to 2 weeks or freeze them for longer storage.
- Allow the truffles to come to room temperature for a few minutes before serving to soften slightly and enhance the flavor.

These assorted holiday truffles are sure to impress your guests and make a wonderful homemade gift for friends and family. Enjoy the decadent flavors and festive spirit of these delightful treats!